GETTING

Housing

SECOND EDITION

DEBBY OUNSTED

trotman

Getting into Housing

This second edition published in 2003
by Trotman and Company Ltd
2 The Green, Richmond, Surrey TW9 1PL

First edition published 2002

© Trotman and Company Limited, Inside Housing and
Housing Corporation 2003

Editorial and Publishing Team
Author Debby Ounsted
Editorial Mina Patria, Editorial Director; Rachel Lockhart, Commissioning Editor; Anya Wilson, Editor; Erin Milliken, Editorial Assistant.
Production Ken Ruskin, Head of Pre-press and Production.
Advertising and Sales Alistair Rogers, Key Accounts Manager;
Mark Tyrell, Sales Executive
Sales and Marketing Deborah Jones, Head of Sales & Marketing
Managing Director Toby Trotman.

British Library Cataloguing in Publication Data
A catalogue record for this book is available from the
British Library.

ISBN 0 85660 941 2

Typeset by Mac Style Ltd, Scarborough, N. Yorkshire
Printed and bound in Great Britain by Printech Europe Ltd, Northampton

CONTENTS

ABOUT THE AUTHOR

Debby Ounsted has worked in housing and local government for 30 years. She tends to keep quiet about her MA in Modern and Medieval Languages, but found her Certificate in Housing Association Finance and her Diploma in Publishing useful in her housing career. She has been Chief Executive of Habinteg Housing Association and of Octavia Hill Housing Trust where she introduced the Investors in People programme that enabled many staff to have better opportunities for personal and career development. Debby has lost track of the number of people she has recruited into housing associations and whose careers she has seen blossom!

She has served on the boards of several housing associations and organisations concerned with disability and for six years chaired the national charity KIDS, which works with children with special needs and their families. She is a Trustee of the Joseph Rowntree Foundation and on the Management Committee of the Mercers Housing Association.

Debby now works as a freelance consultant specialising in organisational change, governance and inspection and lives in London with her husband and two children.

ACKNOWLEDGEMENTS

Many people and organisations have contributed to this book. They share a real enthusiasm for housing as a career and a genuine desire to encourage new, young talent into the sector.

Special thanks are due to David Wright and Kate Murray of *Inside Housing*; Rachel Lockhart at Trotman; Martin Winn, Roger Keller, Jill Goult and Heather Finch and all their colleagues at the Chartered Institute of Housing; Anne Elliott at HACAS Chapman Hendy; Peter Jeffery at Anglia Housing Group; Tom Dacey and Sharon Botting at Southern Housing Group; Adrian Moran, Chris Root and colleagues at the Housing Corporation; Jane Greenoak and Barbara Regnier at the National Housing Federation; Joseph Ogbonna at the Family Housing Association; Gerry Dryden at Heart of England Housing Group; Karen Bennison at Places for People; Sally Jacobson and Dyane Kesto at London and Quadrant Housing Group; Nigel Sprigings at Salford University; David Hewitt at the Association of Residential Management Agents; Jan Mahoney at Stort Valley Housing Association and to many others for sharing their stories about why they came to work in housing. And especially to Jenny Walsh for her skill and patience in turning the raw material into readable form.

Sponsors

We are grateful to our sponsors, the Housing Corporation, Anglia Housing Group, HACAS Chapman Hendy and Southern Housing Group.

The views in this book are those of the author and do not necessarily reflect those of other organisations.

Housing Corporation IGP Database Ref No G0105638

HACASChapmanHendy

GLOSSARY

Affidavit	A legal document signed under oath made as part of court proceedings
ALMO	Arm's-length management organisation. A new company set up by a local authority to manage and maintain its residential properties
Arrears	Rent or other charges owed to a landlord
ASBO	Anti-social behaviour order. A legal process designed to prevent people from continuing to cause disturbance, distress or inconvenience to others
Audit Commission	The Commission through its Housing Inspectorate is responsible, amongst other things, for inspecting and publishing reports on the standards of performance of local authority housing departments and, since April 2003, of RSLs (housing associations)
Chartered Institute of Housing	The professional association for all those working, studying or with an interest in housing (see Chapter 12)
Decent Homes Standard	The minimum standard set by the Government for the quality of all council and housing association homes, which must be achieved by the year 2010
Eviction/Possession proceedings	The legal process of taking back a property from a tenant who has failed to abide by their side of the tenancy agreement (usually because of failure to pay the rent), or of removing someone who has occupied a property illegally, such as a squatter
Fixtures and fittings	Items which are fixed to the property (such as light sockets and radiators) which the landlord is responsible for, as opposed to furniture or other items which usually belong to and are the responsibility of the tenant

Housing benefit	Government-funded financial support towards the cost of housing, payable to people with low or no income
Housing Corporation	The body sponsored by the Government's Office of the Deputy Prime Minister (ODPM) to register, regulate and fund the work of housing associations
Key workers	Public sector employees such as teachers and nurses whose incomes may be too low for them to afford to purchase property within reasonable distance of their workplace
Lettings policy	A description of how people will be selected for particular properties, which usually takes into account the extent of their current housing difficulties
Loss adjusters	Those who assess how much should be paid out by an insurance company on a claim, particularly when the amount claimed is disputed
LSVT associations	Large-scale voluntary transfer associations. These are newly formed housing associations set up to take over the management of properties previously owned by councils
National Housing Federation	The trade body for housing associations that promotes their work and represents their views to government
Nuisance	This is hard to be precise about, but is the term used for annoyance or hurt caused (for which there is sometimes legal remedy – see also ASBO) when one resident or group of residents is disturbed on a regular basis by another, for example by loud music being played late at night, or by regular vandalism
RSL	Registered Social Landlord. Usually known as housing associations, these are bodies set up to provide affordable housing and other services to people on low incomes. They are controlled by voluntary boards and are regulated by the Housing Corporation. They may receive Government funding to help build, renovate and run homes for people who cannot afford housing on the open market

Service charges	Amounts charged to tenants or leaseholders, in addition to the rent, which pay for particular services such as gardening of communal landscaping, electricity used for lighting common halls and stairways, maintenance of lifts in blocks of flats
Specification	The detailed technical description which sets out for a building contractor what work is to be done
Tenancy agreement	The contract signed between landlord and tenant setting out their mutual responsibilities and rights
Tendering	The process of asking several contractors to offer a price for a piece of building work, with a view to making sure that value for money is being obtained
Tenure	The legal term for the method by or conditions on which you occupy your home
Void property	An empty property

FOREWORD

Everyone needs a decent home in which to live. Building and managing housing is a complex profession and there is enormous variety in the kinds of jobs available. From advising people who need a place to live, and managing and maintaining that accommodation, through to those who care for older and vulnerable residents, housing offers a range of jobs that can be both challenging and rewarding. There can be few other jobs where your daily work can transform other people's lives so directly.

Now is an exciting time to start a career in housing. The Government's focus on creating sustainable communities presents challenges to housing professionals in revitalising the older parts of our cities and in helping rural communities to flourish. These represent some of the major challenges which housing professionals now face and where you can really make a difference.

Getting into Housing gives you a taste of the diversity of what housing organisations do. Opportunities for interesting and really enjoyable work abound and training and personal development go with it.

Leaving school? Not sure what to do? Looking for a change of direction or wanting to do something worthwhile? You can really make an impact by choosing a career in housing.

David Butler
The Chartered Institute of Housing

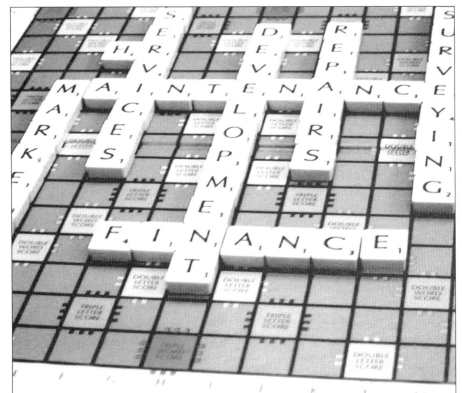

It's your move ...

With over 12,000 properties, Anglia Housing Group is one of the largest providers of affordable homes in the Eastern Region. The Group is committed to providing innovative solutions to meet growing housing need and to improve the quality of our residents' lives by improving the quality of their homes and the communities they live in.

Anglia Housing Group can offer a range of career options. If you are interested in working for an organisation that can offer career development, varied and rewarding roles, flexible working and a range of benefits, visit **www.anglia.org.uk**

Anglia
Housing Group

PREFACE

There's never been a more interesting time to be involved in housing. A leaf through any edition of *Inside Housing*, the leading weekly magazine for housing professionals, proves the point. Each week the magazine demonstrates how much the housing sector is changing and evolving and how much the nation's health, wealth and well-being depends upon its success. With Tony Blair and Gordon Brown taking a personal interest in housing, it's now at the centre stage of political and economic debate.

As a result there can never have been a more interesting time to work in housing. The days when it meant simply collecting rents and ordering repairs are long gone. Those are still important jobs that have to be done but they're carried out as part of a wider drive to improve neighbourhoods, regenerate run-down areas and address the shortage of affordable homes for people on low incomes and key workers such as teachers and police officers.

Move on from *Inside Housing*'s news and feature pages to our appointments section and each week you'll find the evidence of the huge variety of jobs available in housing. Whether it's working for a local authority or a housing association, a campaigning charity, a co-operative or the Office of the Deputy Prime Minister, the range of employers is wide and growing wider. The rewards are good but housing is not just another job where pay and benefits are all that count. It's a job that can provide great personal satisfaction in helping people in need where the results are there to be seen before your eyes.

Inside Housing plays its part in opening the eyes of students and job hunters to the opportunities available in housing. This second edition of *Getting into Housing* is one of the results of that commitment.

Kate Murray
Editor
Inside Housing

Sorted

Want a career with a future? Work for us as a finance, IT, personnel, sales & marketing or PR professional. **Don't fancy getting stuck in an office?** Get out and about managing housing, developing new homes and working with local communities. **Prefer hands-on?** Work at a scheme for older people, or with job seekers in need of support.

It takes a committed team with a huge range of skills to run one of the South East's largest housing associations – which is why we see staff as our best asset.

We'll give you all the training you need when you start, and plenty of support to help develop your career. You'll like our generous holidays and flexible working environment too.

A great start to your working life

INVESTORS IN PEOPLE

For info about current vacancies, phone recruitment on 020 7251 6091.

Or visit our website at **www.shgroup.co.uk**

Southern
Housing
Group

INTRODUCTION – REVITALISING NEIGHBOURHOODS

'Somewhere to live'

We all need somewhere to live. The quality of where we live has a real impact on our lives and on our children's prospects. While most people in Britain own their own homes, 7.5 million people live in rented accommodation. This may be because they prefer renting or because they cannot afford to buy.

Revitalising neighbourhoods

Many new affordable homes are needed in those parts of the country, such as London and the South East, where there are growing opportunities for work, and where house purchase prices are beyond the reach of people on low incomes. Just as great a challenge is the need to bring life back into run-down neighbourhoods, as much in the inner cities as in rural communities. Most people in Britain enjoy a higher standard of living and greater prosperity than ever before, but millions of children and adults are still excluded from this trend. There are some pockets of real deprivation where poor housing and education, lack of jobs and high crime rates lead to serious social stress and a cycle of disadvantage for the people who live there. Housing organisations are now at the heart of partnerships with residents, helping change the face of poorer Britain and putting real opportunity for a better quality of life within reach of all.

Creativity, flair and drive

The Government is determined to transform public services and it needs people with creativity, flair and drive to meet this challenge.

The range of jobs available and of skills and qualities needed to play a part in this transformation is enormous. This book is about the sort of

1

work involved in helping people get suitable housing and improving the quality of life for people living in less well-off areas, about the kinds of people you might work with and the career paths you might follow.

WHAT DO WE MEAN BY 'HOUSING'?

Local councils and housing associations own 5.3 million properties that they let, often at a rent well below the private sector rent level, to people who are on their lists or are homeless. Planning and building homes, letting to tenants, collecting the rent, doing the repairs, solving neighbourhood problems, helping families who need to move and keeping estates clean and tidy is a surprisingly big and complicated undertaking.

Many estates and housing schemes built by local authorities and housing associations are lovely places to live, with good local services, and are popular with new applicants. But parts of some towns and cities have very poor housing. In some localities it is hard to find people willing to rent the homes that become available. The quality of life and the prospects for people who live in these areas can be dismal. A mixture of things can make a neighbourhood go downhill: lack of work, below-average schools, bad public transport, lack of places for recreation, fear of crime, poor security and so on. In some parts of the country the 'housing market' has collapsed both in the privately owned and in the rented sector; no one wants to purchase or to rent homes in run-down areas. People who can afford to get out may vote with their feet. It can be a real downward spiral for those who are left behind and they may need extra help and support. By contrast, some places are housing hotspots where there are large numbers of applicants for properties available from councils and housing associations, where private rents are out of reach for people on low incomes and house prices are far too high for first-time buyers. And in many cities, areas of high and low demand are only a few miles apart, which can create serious social tensions.

Helping to tackle these major problems is some of the most challenging and rewarding work around today. Where major city regeneration projects are under way tenants often have to move so that extensive modernisation can be carried out, redundant buildings demolished and new community facilities, shops and offices provided. This means arranging temporary moves, bringing the danger of breaking up well-established community networks, with all the disruption which that entails. Rebuilding those communities, working closely with residents and bringing new investment in to revitalise neighbourhoods is immensely satisfying work. Good liaison between all the different bodies concerned is essential – regional government and local councils, businesses and banks, schools, health and education workers, social services and the police all have a part to play. And obtaining grants and loans from all sorts of different government and private financiers to do the work is a job in itself.

Meanwhile there are many neighbourhoods where 'prevention' is what matters most – making sure that there is enough intelligent investment both in the buildings and in the community to prevent everything from collapsing if the local economy is put under pressure, for example if a big local employer moves out.

Homelessness and the threat of becoming homeless remains a serious problem. Councils have a duty in law to find homes for people who are vulnerable and who have become homeless through circumstances outside their control. Many people need more than just a roof over their heads: older people may need occasional help, or to be cared for on a regular basis as they become more frail; people with special needs may need to have support and help available if they are to cope with living independently.

This whole enterprise is often given the shorthand title 'social housing' or the more upbeat name 'affordable housing'. Around 115,000 people are employed by housing associations in England in providing and managing such housing, and this number is set to double in the next five years. The overall figures when you add in people employed by councils, in housing benefit administration, by the private sector, by big institutions like universities which own student accommodation, and so on, is estimated at around 650,000 people. So you can see that job opportunities abound.

A total of 28,500 new homes to rent are being built with the help of public grants in 2003/4. There are also many private landlords, who let their property without any government subsidy. Decent housing for everyone is at the heart of public social policy, because it is recognised as having a fundamental part to play in individual health and well-being, together with the more talked-about education and health services. But whereas house prices are always in the public eye, rented housing receives little media attention, so it has often been overlooked as a career by people who want to have a social purpose in their work.

An exciting time to get involved

It is an exciting time to get involved in housing with all the changes and improvements that are happening. In February 2003 the Government issued the Sustainable Communities Plan, setting out its strong backing for councils and housing associations. Extra resources are being allocated to make a real impact on run-down neighbourhoods and to help reinvigorate communities, allowing them to take more control over the improvements which are needed. The 'New Deal for Communities' helps bring all sorts of different resources into the most disadvantaged neighbourhoods. Plenty of new homes will be built too. 'Key workers' such as teachers and nurses will have the opportunity to get on the property ladder. The National Housing Federation has launched a new campaign with the strapline 'In business for neighbourhoods' to improve the way housing associations are thought of. All councils must now make and publish a plan to show how they will make sure that all homes in their area meet the 'Decent Homes' standard. Over the next few years all this 'regeneration' and new housing work will have a high profile and there will be resources to help fund dramatic improvements. Councils and housing associations will be working closely with local residents, to make their future prospects brighter.

Green issues and sustainable housing

There is also a real interest in 'green' issues that relate to housing. International political concerns about the effects of climate change and the need for sustainability have made a real impact. Construction methods and materials need to be chosen for their environmental suitability. Making sure that new homes are energy efficient and use materials wisely is only part of the task. Finding ways of using new technology to make homes more convenient is a priority. Making sure people can afford to light and heat their homes is very important for people on low incomes. Making homes accessible for people who have physical disabilities has become more important as the population ages too. All existing homes are meant to reach the 'Decent Homes' standard by 2010. In addition, housing organisations are investing in the people side of communities as well the bricks and mortar.

Homes built today are going to have to last. So everyone has an interest in improving the environment as well as making sure homes are well built, and this includes areas where there are many council and housing association homes.

'I WORK IN HOUSING'

When people say 'I work in housing,' they may be doing anything from helping a homeless family into their first permanent home, collecting rent, or organising a huge renovation programme in a tower block.

Many black and ethnic-minority families are poorly housed compared with most of the rest of the population. There are a number of housing associations led by people from ethnic minorities who recognise the special challenges of ensuring real equality of opportunity for people who may be disadvantaged because of their ethnic origin. If you join an organisation with housing in a multiracial area you will be working to develop better links and relationships between community groups.

You might take a job in a rural community, helping to provide homes that local people, perhaps on a low agricultural wage, can afford. Housing and economic stress can be acute in country areas, especially when transport links are poor and buying a home is pricey. You might be employed by a council to work with private landlords helping them improve their homes. Or you might be on the frontline, working in customer care. Whether you want to work in one of the big conurbations, or whether you prefer the country, you will find there are great opportunities for getting into housing as a career. What is shared by everyone involved in housing is the common purpose of helping people to get a decent place to live and helping them to enjoy their home as long as they stay.

Are you about to leave school?

This wide variety in the kinds of jobs available means a wide range of qualities, skills, competencies and qualifications are needed. Many of the skills that school-leavers or students develop while doing holiday jobs can be a good grounding for work in housing, for example the ability to communicate well with people at all levels, the ability to do tasks on time and to see tasks through to the end.

Are you a graduate?

There are many graduate entrants to housing who have a relevant degree, but some, including those in senior positions, come from completely different disciplines. There are plenty of opportunities for interested graduates to move across. Chapter 12 gives more details.

Thinking of a career change?

You may be reading this book because you are thinking about a career move in later life, or going back to work after a career break. One of the best things about housing is that it welcomes incomers from different backgrounds. You are less likely to find that your age is an issue when looking for a new job. This is because housing organisations are generally scrupulous in applying best recruitment practice when looking for new staff. They want the best person for the job, and they recognise the importance of life experience in a career that is essentially about people.

You might be an accountant in the City, or in IT or in marketing, or a surveyor, and you might feel that you are being ground down by the profit motive. You may be working in a corporate services function, like human resources. All housing organisations need corporate services, just as much as do private companies. In Chapter 9 there are plenty of examples of interesting and worthwhile jobs in other professions that play an essential part in the success of housing organisations. Being able to transfer your experience and skills into this enjoyable sector is well worth considering.

CAREER PROSPECTS

Prospects for a satisfying career in housing have never been better. Property Housing and Facilities Management Skills is the Government's skills agency for the housing sector. In the spring of 2002 it launched a workforce development plan, commissioned by the Department for Education and Skills, which sets out what action is needed to recruit, retain and develop a suitably buoyant workforce for housing in the 21st century, not just for subsidised rented housing but for private renting and managing different kinds of rented housing as well. Their website at www.housingpotential.com is well worth visiting to find out more.

Training and career development

Councils and housing associations are generally keen to help all staff develop their careers and there is often support available for a variety of courses, from HNC through to postgraduate and Chartered Institute of Housing professional qualifications. Many employers have the Investors in People badge, which means they really are committed to giving employees the best possible chance to get a lot out of their work. Of all staff, 9.7 per cent come from black and minority ethnic backgrounds and housing organisations are committed to offering equal opportunities to all.

In-house training and external courses are usually provided for staff. There is a lot of job mobility between employers. Someone might start work as a trainee with a housing association, move on to a council's housing department and move on later to a government body or another association on promotion. Some employers have only a handful of staff, others have a cast of thousands. So there are great opportunities for working in different parts of the country and getting a variety of experience.

CASE STUDY

Sharon Botting, Area Manager, Southern Housing Group

Sharon Botting began her career in housing straight after leaving school in 1976, when she joined Southern Housing Group as an Office Junior in the Horsham office.

'If I'm honest, I was just looking for a job and this came up,' she admits. 'I wasn't sure what I wanted at 17 – but I haven't looked back since!'

After gaining experience in the office, Sharon took on the role of Housing Assistant, offering administrative support to the housing management team. Later, she progressed to arrears work. 'I shared an office with the person keeping the ledger and journal of rents paid. It was all done by hand in those days!' she recalls.

Sharon's next post was working as Assistant to the Housing Manager, which she followed by becoming a Housing Officer. 'I dealt with a huge patch in London and right down to Horsham. We were "generic" – we handled everything to do with housing management and arrears. Later, the Group took on some retirement leasehold properties – for retired home owners – which changed my patch slightly and meant we were handling leasehold issues as well.'

By the end of the 1990s, Sharon's experience saw her promoted to Senior Management Officer and she spent around five years managing four patch managers and an administrator. Then in March 2003, her role altered following restructuring in the organisation, when the Group introduced a one-stop Service Centre as the first point of contact for residents. 'I'm now an Area Manager,' Sharon explains. 'I have more staff to manage and more management responsibility – for example, I now have maintenance staff under my umbrella.'

'I manage a team of eight staff: two administrators; three patch managers who manage our more dispersed stock; a Neighbourhood Housing Manager who works from an estate office in Bracknell and does more resident participation work; a maintenance surveyor and an inspector and their administrator.'

It's a varied and interesting job, which suits Sharon down to the ground. 'I love dealing with people – trying to solve their problems and help them.' But she admits it isn't always plain sailing. 'Unfortunately, the higher up the ladder you go, the more complaints you deal with! But there's satisfaction in sorting them out and getting it right. Even if you can't always give people what they want, you can soften the blow.'

YOU can make a real difference

Housing appeals as a career because young people can make a real practical impact from the very start. As soon as they try to leave home, school-leavers and students understand at first hand how hard it is to find a place to live and what a difference good housing makes. Housing employers often look for potential, rather than long track records, and are genuinely committed to being equal opportunities employers, seeking to get the best from their workforce. Staff in housing teams are enthusiastic and energetic, enjoying the challenge of a practical job with a serious social purpose.

HOW THIS BOOK IS ARRANGED

Because all councils and associations have different numbers of properties to look after, the way in which the work is arranged will vary from place to place. The job titles also differ from employer to employer. For example, a customer services adviser in one place might be doing much the same as a repairs assistant in another. Policies and priorities also vary tremendously, so this book should be taken as a general guide only. But each job will have a written explanation of what the work and its responsibilities are. This is usually called a job description. It's important to look at what it says in the job description or job brief. There will also be a 'person specification' which describes the kind of qualities, skills or experience applicants for the job are likely to need. It's important to look at what the job description says rather than just the title of the job, and at the person specification when deciding whether or not a particular post is for you.

The different chapters in this book describe the different sorts of functions there are to be performed. If you work in Scotland, Wales or Northern Ireland the terminology, funding and administrative structures will be slightly different to those in England. Devolution to all parts of the UK will mean that changes will continue to be introduced. The appropriate office of the Chartered Institute of Housing, or the national equivalents of the Housing Corporation in England (addresses are given at the back of this book), can give you more information. But you will find the jobs described broadly available from landlords – both public and private – throughout the UK.

A word on **jargon**. As in most professions, people in housing love talking in jargon, using shorthand for complicated terms and initials for long-winded names. We don't realise we're doing it most of the time! Although this book has tried to simplify and explain things, there is also a glossary on pages vi and vii that should help.

CASE STUDY

Sally Jacobson is the Personnel and Training Director at London and Quadrant Housing Group. Sally moved into housing from the NHS 15 years ago. She says 'What could be more fundamental to health than good housing, and where else could you make such a difference every day of your working life? When you work in housing you know that you are playing a part in transforming lives. That is true whether you work on the front line or in finance, or in personnel and training like myself. We are all part of the team. It's fantastically busy and we encourage anyone who wants a satisfying career and to make a real contribution to give it a try.'

BACKGROUND – AN INDUSTRY OVERVIEW

Before thinking about what's involved in working in housing, you need to have an idea about what the different kinds of housing organisations are, how they are run and who they are accountable to for the quality of what they do. The thing to remember is that there are huge changes afoot, with residents as 'customers' becoming ever more involved and influential in deciding how things should be done.

WHAT IS COUNCIL HOUSING?

Local authorities or councils are run by elected councillors who normally represent a political party. The party with the most councillors decides what is to be spent on which activities each year. Councils employ paid staff and may be one of the biggest employers in their area. They are responsible for a wide variety of services. These can include:

- education
- libraries and leisure
- social services
- refuse collection and street cleaning
- environmental matters such as air and noise pollution control
- planning
- licensing shops, pubs and restaurants

and, of course, housing.

They have an important role in forming the strategies for what is to be done in their area, through local strategic partnerships.

They collect a council tax from every household and rates from each business in their area and these, together with income from people who use their services and money from the Government, go to cover the cost of what they do. They administer housing benefit, which helps people with no or low incomes to pay for their housing. They also provide and manage permanent houses and flats to rent, and must give help to people who are homeless. Council housing has to meet the standards approved by the Audit Commission's Housing Inspectorate who examine the quality of what is done each year, compare the performance of one council with another, give a grade and suggest areas for improvement. These reports are published on the Audit Commission's website, so are well worth looking at if you are thinking about a career in local government.

All councils now have to demonstrate to Government how they are going to bring all the homes they own up to the Decent Homes standard. Some councils still run their housing directly themselves. They may decide to raise money through the Private Finance Initiative to modernise the properties. Some have passed their properties over to be run by housing associations (LSVT associations; see next section) after a tenants' vote. In some organisations tenants, through tenant management organisations, are in charge of ensuring that the standards of housing management are up to scratch. Councils can set up new bodies called arm's length management organisations (ALMOs) to manage their homes, as long as they provide good or excellent standards of service to residents. These new ALMOs can obtain extra money from Government to help pay for repairs and modernisation.

WHAT IS A HOUSING ASSOCIATION?

Housing associations are independent voluntary organisations that, unlike private companies, do not exist to make a profit for shareholders. Their main purpose is to provide housing for people in need. Many associations are registered as charities. They are governed by a board or committee of management whose members are usually not paid for the work they do. They are volunteers. They are likely to bring to bear expertise from their own working lives to help guide the work of their association. More and more associations have residents on their boards who have direct experience of the quality of their landlord's work. Information about joining a housing association board is in Chapter 9.

The board oversees the policy and direction of the association's work and usually employs paid staff to carry it out. The money they need to build houses and do their other work comes partly from the rents they collect, partly from the Government via a body called the Housing Corporation, in England, and partly from private loans. More than 2,000 associations are registered with the Housing Corporation, meaning their standards of work have been checked and they are thought fit to receive Government support.

There are about 500 larger, active associations that are building new homes and are involved in regeneration work. Some associations are huge, with more than 50,000 homes; they work all over the country, employing thousands of staff. Others have just a handful of homes and one or two employees.

Some are based in just one or two boroughs and might be involved in other activities as well as housing, such as community work and employment and training initiatives. Some specialise in helping particular groups of vulnerable people, such as frail elderly people, or young adults with learning disabilities. Many work in towns where the population includes people from black and minority ethnic groups. Many associations are very small, and might for example run just one long-established almshouse or a hostel in a rural village.

Many councils are transferring their properties across to be managed by new housing associations set up specifically for that purpose. These are known as LSVT associations (large-scale voluntary transfer associations). They concentrate on working with tenants in the district to upgrade the former council housing stock and look for new local housing and regeneration possibilities.

Housing associations have clear guidelines for their work and are regulated by the Housing Corporation. Every three years or so they are inspected by the Audit Commission's Housing Inspectorate, as councils are. They are given an assessment for the quality of service they provide and for whether they are likely to improve. The reports are made public, so if you are going for a job at a housing association you can look for their inspection report on the Housing Corporation or the Audit Commission's website.

DIFFERENT KINDS OF HOUSING ORGANISATIONS

You may have heard of other names for organisations involved in housing – cooperatives, housing action trusts, tenant management organisations, housing companies and arm's-length management organisations, for example.

There are also plenty of housing jobs within the private sector, working as a managing agent for small landlords or institutions that own property which is let or leased privately and not built with the help of public money. The legislation is different but the skills are relevant. Another obviously related career is within estate agency, selling homes to people who prefer to purchase rather than rent their homes.

Within the council and housing association sector there is a great deal of scope for learning about different forms of home ownership. The Government is keen to see more people enabled to buy a place of their own. Council tenants and others have had the 'right to buy' the property they live in for some years, which means that there may be a mixture of tenures within one group of properties. 'Tenure' is the word used to describe how you occupy your home, whether as a tenant, freeholder or leaseholder. In blocks of flats some people may have weekly tenancies and others may have purchased a long lease for say 99 years (with the right to sell on). Managing blocks where residents have different tenures is especially demanding and is a good training ground if you want to work in the private sector later.

Many housing associations offer different forms of home ownership aimed at people with relatively low incomes but who want to get a stake in the value of their home, for example shared ownership for key workers and leasehold schemes for elderly people.

It is beyond the scope of this book to go into detail on how all these different organisations arrange their work. But the types of jobs described will crop up in different guises and with different names in most housing organisations. All offer examples of the real potential for exciting and challenging work in housing today, and learning your way round in one organisation will prepare you well to develop your career further in another, as so many of the skills you will learn are transferable.

PART ONE: CAREER CHOICES

CASE STUDY

Jan Mahoney, Housing Officer, Stort Valley Housing Association

Jan Mahoney started as a Housing Assistant for Stort Valley Housing Association (a member of Anglia Housing Group) in 2002 and has recently been promoted to Housing Officer.

Jan works in an area of the country that has recently been identified by the government as a key growth area. This means that these areas will benefit from regeneration and thousands of new homes are being planned, of which many will be owned and managed by organisations like Anglia Housing Group. Prior to working in housing, Jan worked within retail management for Thorntons, leaving to become a full-time mother in 1996.

'I enjoyed retail management, but the hours are long and you're always on call. With four children it's hard to go out at 3am to deal with a burglar alarm. But Stort Valley is very understanding as an employer. It's 100% better than the private sector.'

Jan answered a job advert that stressed the benefits to be gained by working in housing, rather than concentrating on narrow definitions of the skills and qualifications required. She now recognises that she bought some real transferable skills from her previous experiences.

'Managing a Thornton's chocolate shop and working as a housing assistant are similar in that they are both customer-focused, so I was able to utilise my people skills – you need to enjoy working with people, and get pleasure out of giving excellent customer service. It's 70% people skills to 30% office skills.'

With a young family, Jan was also attracted by the flexitime working arrangements. Since working in the sector Jan has identified the many learning opportunities available which in turn has opened up an entirely new avenue in her new career in housing.

'Working in housing has given me a lot of benefits, flexitime is vital in my other role as a mother. On-the-job training has been essential and although I have now been working within housing for over a year, I am still learning and this helps to keep the job interesting. Most of all I get a lot of job satisfaction, I like to go home at the end of the day with a sense of achievement. There is no better feeling than when you have helped someone stay in their home.'

Chapter 1
WORKING IN NEIGHBOURHOOD MANAGEMENT

Both councils and housing associations employ staff in a variety of positions to carry out the complicated job of managing property. The emphasis nowadays is on the quality of the service given to the residents and whether the service is getting better year by year.

So the phrase used to describe this work, housing management, has often been replaced by 'tenant services', or the much wider term 'neighbourhood management', indicating that people and communities, rather than just the bricks and mortar, are at the heart of things.

Here are some of the functions that are commonly performed by the tenant services or neighbourhood management department. The term 'assistant' (for example lettings assistant) is frequently used for someone doing fairly routine administrative duties. 'Officers' (for example housing officer) may be responsible for a wider range of duties and more involved in decision-making. Teams of officers will usually be headed by a manager who is likely to be professionally qualified, and in turn managers will report to the director of the whole department.

LETTINGS OR ALLOCATIONS

The responsibilities include:

- Keeping up to date the list of people waiting for homes.
- Keeping a register of which tenants would like or need to transfer to a different property, or to move to a property owned by a different landlord altogether, or to swap their home with a tenant of another social landlord (called a Mutual Exchange).
- When properties become empty, deciding with colleagues, in line with the agreed policy, who should be offered the vacancy, taking into account the number of bedrooms and the location and comparing that

17

with what people both need and would like. There are also schemes now to give more choice to applicants.

- Planning who is going to move into newly built properties that are being occupied for the first time.
- Liaising with the local council, which will keep a list of people seeking housing in the district and who may have priority for having their names put forward to local housing associations. (Most associations sign a nominations agreement with their local council to offer a proportion of their homes to people on the council list; this is in exchange for getting public grants.)
- Liaising with other housing organisations, especially where your tenants want to move to a different part of the country or need a size of property that your organisation does not have available.
- Keeping required records of who has been housed and where.
- Monitoring how long it takes to relet empty property – keeping the length of time a property has been empty ('void') as short as possible is a high priority for landlords.
- Feeding back to the design team what tenants like about their homes, and what sort of property is in great demand (e.g. detached three-bed houses with gardens).
- Liaising with other agencies such as social services if the person being housed needs support. This could include attending a case conference where a number of agencies come together to co-ordinate how they can work together to help an applicant.

While it can be very satisfying to find a property that really matches what the applicant wants, working in Lettings can be stressful where there is high demand for social housing, because you are often seen as a gatekeeper, whose main job is to say 'No'.

By contrast, in some parts of the country particularly in the Midlands and the North, some areas have become so undesirable that it is hard to let properties at all. Or it may be that the design and facilities in the property have become outmoded (e.g. bed-sits with shared bathrooms). Private flats nearby may have lower rents. Lettings staff have to keep an eye out for signs that this is beginning to happen. Of course there is the immediate problem that an empty flat does not generate any rental income for the landlord. But a bigger concern is the other problems empty flats can bring, such as dereliction, vandalism and squatting.

Lettings staff often need to be imaginative in finding new ways of making homes appeal, and there are many experiments going on to make the whole process more attractive and effective, giving greater choice to tenants. Staff will also help the landlord identify which properties need modernising and updating if they are to continue being acceptable to new generations of tenants.

Experiments are also being conducted to find ways of helping communities remain stable when vacancies come up or new estates are built. Community Lettings Policies mean that rather than just give a property to the person at the top of the list, the landlord can consider other reasons for offering someone housing in a particular locality: they might have long-standing family connections, or they might want to move into the area for job reasons, or the estate might have lots of young families already, so priority might be given to older couples or single people. Whenever possible, landlords are encouraged to give applicants a choice of properties, because if people have some choice over where they are housed, they are more likely to settle and be happy there. So working in Lettings is interesting, and weighing up all the factors can be tricky.

Skills and qualities

- good communication
- excellent administrative skills with an eye for detail
- fair-mindedness
- sensitivity inside a tough skin!

A day in the life of a Housing Officer

8am In early to get rent-chasing letters out to Ms B and Mr Z and check yesterday's rent printout. Ouch, my arrears are up this week.

9am Bike over to visit Mrs A, new tenant who doesn't speak English. She needs help with understanding how to fill out her benefit claim. Her grandson acts as interpreter. Turns out she's also worried that stairwells are dark. Remind caretaker to adjust timing on the central lights.

10am Back at office; I'm on a Best Value review group. We are looking at ways of improving how we do things in

---

consultation with our 'customers', the tenants. We're thinking about our service charges. That's the money we have to charge to tenants on top of their rents for things such as communal heating and lighting, caretaking and lifts. If we can streamline the administration and give more accurate details to tenants there'll be fewer complaints and it'll be easier to collect the income we need to cover the costs. It makes sense really.

12 noon Sandwich man arrives. I'll get a cheese and tomato and a Mars bar to keep me going; I'm in court this afternoon on an eviction. Bump into the repairs administrator in reception. Remind him Mrs H needs her heating fixed urgently; she's coming out of hospital this afternoon.

Ring the social worker about Mr S. The neighbours say he isn't looking after himself and there's a funny smell coming from his flat. Arrange a visit with the environmental health officer to see if there's a serious problem.

2pm Go to court. Luckily I remembered to change into my suit. See some of my friends who are also doing my housing course. Coursework has helped me to understand the legal side of housing better. We didn't think we needed a solicitor on this case as it was straightforward. Judge seems quite sympathetic given the high level of arrears, but I think the fact I did the affidavit so thoroughly helps. Tenant doesn't show up. I think he's done a bunk. We are granted possession. Wonder what'll happen to him. Do diary note to get the flat cleared and secured.

4.30pm Pop in to see Mrs H on my way back to the office; fantastic; the heating engineers are just leaving; her daughter's there waiting for the ambulance to bring her back. I promise to check everything's OK with the home care team tomorrow.

Back at the office, lettings team are pleased about the court result, because the man who's gone was taking up a three-bed house with a garden: they're pure gold dust to the lettings people.

5.30pm Tenants' association meeting on one of my estates tonight. Should be OK now that noisy tenant has moved away.

> Ooh look, I didn't have time to eat the Mars bar. Funny thing, I once thought of applying to work for them when I was a student. Lots of my friends did. Glad I didn't; housing's more exciting than chocolate. A good day really; several satisfied customers; computer didn't break down; and I'm off on day release tomorrow so I can sleep in.

HOUSING MANAGEMENT – OR TENANT SERVICES

This team's work is at the centre of what every housing organisation does. Staff in housing or estate management are likely to be responsible for:

- 'Signing up', which means going through the tenancy agreement with new tenants, making sure they understand what the responsibilities in it imply, sorting out keys, gas and electricity. Usually a detailed tenants' handbook is given out too.
- Helping them move in if needed.
- Arranging furniture if needed.
- Helping people who are applying for housing benefit complete the forms and checking that they understand what their benefit entitlement is.
- Checking that people have settled in and that they know how to handle the basic fixtures in the property, such as the central heating.
- Making sure they know how to report repairs and also which repairs they are expected to do themselves.
- Making sure that rent is paid regularly and on time.
- Making arrangements to collect arrears, including giving benefits advice to help maximise people's incomes.
- Liaising with social services or voluntary support agencies if an individual needs any special kind of support day to day, for example because of mental ill health or because they are increasingly vulnerable through old age.
- Usually managing the caretakers based on the estates, and making sure they have all the supplies they need to keep the surroundings and the communal parts of buildings clean and tidy.

- Responding to complaints from tenants if neighbours cause nuisance or disturbance; this could range from the noise from toddlers' feet in the upstairs flat through late-night rowdy parties to drug dealing or other criminal activity.
- Working through the legal system if a tenant has to be evicted; this is only likely to arise if there are serious and persistent arrears, serious nuisance, or harassment or other criminal behaviour.
- Getting feedback from tenants about the services provided and involving tenants in how their homes are managed. This may mean working closely with residents' and tenants' associations, meeting groups of tenants out of hours to hear their ideas on how things could be done differently and better. Housing organisations review their procedures regularly, and compare their quality and cost with others, often through a process called 'best value'. Housing staff are often closely involved in these reviews.
- Working closely with the development teams when new homes are being designed.

Skills and qualities

You need to be well organised and also a good organiser of others; scrupulously fair-minded, tactful and discreet; firm; robust enough to cope with stressful situations, for which you often can find no answer.

CASE STUDY

Susie started as a temp on reception at a medium-sized housing association in West London, covering the job for a woman who was on maternity leave. She'd previously worked as a cashier in a bank. She found her training in customer care from the bank really useful in her new position.

She was then asked to cover the post of a housing assistant who was on extended sick leave, and made such a success of it that she applied for and got the job permanently when the post-holder decided not to come back to work. She then studied for a BTEC, being allowed day-release, and meanwhile was promoted to housing officer. She failed one of her papers first time, but persisted and successfully completed the course while she was on six months' maternity leave herself. Although she lived more than an hour away from the office she decided to continue commuting to her job when she came back from maternity leave, but kept an eye open for other possibilities closer to home. This was a hard time for her, juggling the day-to-day housing officer visits to sites across London with the need to meet her childcare commitments.

The association that employed her then merged with another association and Susie was promoted to a senior position, which was more managerial and office-based. She was given the chance to train in the staff managerial skills she needed to develop and has much more flexibility over her day-to-day working arrangements, so as well as gaining a promotion she has also made life a bit easier on the childcare front.

Chapter 2
THE FRONT LINE: CUSTOMER SERVICES

RECEPTION WORK

First impressions of any kind of organisation are important. How customers are treated on the phone and when they visit the office affects significantly what they think of the organisation. Courtesy, thoughtfulness and efficiency from the receptionist who sits at the front desk create a positive image. Housing organisations usually vie with the best to provide a welcoming, fresh and professional front-desk service.

Many councils and larger housing associations now deal with tenants mainly by phone. Many use call centres (sometimes called customer service centres). The staff answering the phone may be based miles away from where the tenant lives. However, new technology makes it possible, as in other service industries, to deal with most of the routine requests – ordering a repair or checking a rent account – by phone. More complex questions will be referred on to the appropriate housing staff, who are more likely to be based in a local office.

'Customers' in the social housing world are a mixture of people. They may be families desperate for a place to live. They may be tenants who need urgent repairs to their home. They may be elderly people feeling threatened by noisy youths or locals who hold the landlord responsible for everything that goes on in the neighbourhood. They may be other professionals such as social workers, or applicants coming for a job interview.

All housing organisations, councils and associations alike, have daily communication with other official bodies, such as Government departments, and Members of Parliament and councillors. Many other people will be in regular phone and personal contact: maintenance contractors, IT installers, delivery people, solicitors, architects, surveyors – the list is endless.

All of these people will be affected by the way they are treated by the person in the council or association they first have contact with. If the receptionist is abrupt or fails to pass on a message, or if the person at the call centre who answers the phone is rude or patronising, then the customer will go away with the opinion that everyone who works for that organisation is like that. Equally, a good experience will create a satisfied customer. Research shows that we are far more likely to tell other people about a bad experience we have had than a good one! So it is vital that the customer approach is as positive, welcoming and efficient as it can be.

Even though much communication now is by email or direct phone line rather than through a switchboard, the bulk of first contact is still through the front line staff. The position really matters.

Arrangements differ, depending on the size of the organisation. A smaller place might have only one or two staff dealing with phone enquiries, handling all reception duties and sometimes doing word processing and central administration as well. Administration could include:

- answering calls and managing the switchboard
- taking responsibility for opening and distributing the post
- getting the evening post out
- ensuring that there are up-to-date supplies of rent books and other documentation needed by tenants
- arranging courier deliveries of important documents
- keeping track of keys to homes available to be let or where building work is being done
- taking details of repairs that need to be done
- keeping track of the office diary, knowing who is where when
- welcoming guests, keeping the visitors log, escorting people to meetings.

In larger housing organisations, there may be much bigger teams using sophisticated IT, acting as customer services officers who are trained to deal on the phone with a wide range of enquiries and problems. Technology may have been installed which makes it easy to identify where a caller lives, what outstanding or previous problems they may have asked you to deal with, what make of equipment is installed in the home, so that it is easier to order spare parts when repairs are needed –

there's a lengthy list of useful information computer systems can hold to make the service more efficient.

REPAIRS ORDERING AND ADMINISTRATION

One of the main differences between being a tenant and owning your own place is that a tenant is not usually responsible for repairs to the property: that is the landlord's job.

Once the tenancy agreement has been signed and the new family has moved in, repairs are sometimes their only reason to contact the landlord. More than any other aspect of the services offered, the quality of the maintenance affects people's opinion of the landlord. There is nothing that sours public opinion like poor maintenance, no matter what the reason for it.

Councils and housing associations need to keep their properties in good repair. Not only are they legally obliged to do so, but they want to make sure tenants have a property that is in decent condition. If major faults – such as leaks from water tanks or slipped slates on the roof – are left to fester, eventually the damage will be significant. So landlords want to offer a quick and efficient repairs service.

Social landlords publish the standard amount of time it should take for repair work to be done: usually an emergency, such as a broken front door, might be dealt with on the same day; urgent repairs, such as restoring hot water, done within 3 days; and routine repairs, such as to fencing or a loose window sash, within 28 days.

The administrators or customer services advisers will usually be responsible for:

- placing an order for routine repairs to be done by an approved contractor or an in-house operator
- deciding if a surveyor should visit the property and inspect the problem
- making arrangements for a builder to get in
- following up the progress on the work (the contractor may have to wait for spare parts, and the tenant will want to be reassured that the job has not been forgotten)

- signing off the job when it is completed so that the invoice can be processed and paid
- recording and monitoring statistics
- checking that the tenant is satisfied with the work done.

Skills and qualities

As well as having a genuine desire to help people sort out problems you need to be a good listener – able to probe to get accurate information. You must enjoy the real practicalities of learning how a house and its fixtures and fittings are put together. And you need to be a terrier, determined to see the detail right through to the end. A good telephone manner and a bit of personal charm may smooth the job along too.

Chapter 3
MAINTENANCE AND SURVEYING

Housing is all about providing homes for people, and bricks and mortar are fundamental to this. The biggest asset of any landlord – aside from the staff, that is! – is likely to be the properties he or she owns. Quite apart from the need to keep the home warm and dry for the benefit of the people who live there, a landlord needs to keep property in good repair in order to maintain its value. A house with a leaking roof, rattling window frames and rising damp is going to be less valuable than one in decent condition. This is just as true for a small private landlord as for a council with thousands of properties.

Chapter 2 explained the job of the administrators who take calls from residents asking for repairs to be done. Working closely with the administrators are the technical people, the surveyors whose job it is to diagnose the causes of major problems, decide on the cure and make sure the building contractors do the work well.

Some larger housing organisations, especially councils, employ their own in-house labour force of tradesmen with the different skills needed to keep their properties in good repair. They may offer training, leading to nationally recognised qualifications.

Repairs are usually described as either 'day-to-day', 'cyclical' or 'major works'.

DAY-TO-DAY REPAIRS

These routine repairs will not usually need a technical expert to work out what needs to be done. Examples would be central heating problems – usually dealt with direct by a qualified engineer – a slipped roof slate or a faulty lock. Often a surveyor will only be called in to carry out inspections on a percentage of the completed jobs, just to check that the repair work has been well done and that the tenant is satisfied with the way the contractor has dealt with the problem.

It is now quite common for larger landlords to set up what are called 'partnering arrangements' with a larger contractor who assumes the responsibility for all repairs at agreed rates. This can mean that the contractor builds up good knowledge over time of the different kinds of properties, what sorts of things tend to go wrong, and how to fix faults in an efficient way. The contractor and the landlord can develop a better long-term working relationship, each understanding what the other wants to achieve and what barriers if any are thwarting improvement of the service. The cost of administering repairs can also be reduced as fewer small jobs are put out to a range of different contractors.

CYCLICAL WORK

In order to keep a property weatherproof, landlords are well advised to redecorate the outside every five years. Other routine tasks can be done at the same time, for example checking the pointing (the mortar between the bricks); making sure gutters aren't clogged with leaves; seeing that locks, doors and windows are easy to open and close; checking that the paving of any paths, and any fencing or walls around the property, are in good condition.

Surveyors will usually be involved in drawing up what is called the 'specification', describing the work that needs to be done. They will ask various contractors to give their price for doing the job. This is called 'tendering'. Then they will appoint a firm – usually the one offering the lowest price – to do the work. A contract will be drawn up and a timetable agreed and the surveyor will oversee the work.

It is a skilled job to work out what needs to be done at 'cyclical' time. It makes sense to group properties together for economies of scale, especially if scaffolding is to be used. On the other hand, there is little point in doing equal amounts of repainting if some properties show less signs of wear and tear than others.

There is also a special skill involved in liaising with residents whenever contractors are working on their property. People like to be involved in choosing things such as colour schemes, but sometimes there are conflicting preferences. Inevitably things sometimes go wrong – window panes can get broken by scaffolding; windows may be painted shut; parts of a house can be overlooked. The surveyor in charge therefore needs to be able to explain what is being done and be tactful and courteous, often acting as an intermediary between the tenant, the contractor and the landlord, who, after all, is paying the bills with the tenants' rent.

MAJOR REPAIRS AND IMPROVEMENTS

Surveyors are key players when it comes to significant repairs. All components on a property have a natural 'life'. Electrical wiring becomes out of date; plasterwork gets damaged; mortar fails, letting dampness in; kitchen units fall apart; roofs start to sag and slates and tiles crack. It does not always make sense to go on patching up piecemeal.

Diagnosis is a highly complex job. Anyone can see that a wall is damp, but it takes a person with skill, knowledge and experience to work out whether this is due to rising damp, condensation or damp penetrating from outside, or a leak. In each case the cure will be different. Professionally qualified staff will almost always be in charge of maintenance teams, but there are often posts for trainees who want to qualify or for people who have started work in the building industry but want to move across.

Rising standards of living and higher expectations mean that regular investment is needed. This not only improves the quality of life for residents but also protects and might increase the value of the asset owned by the landlord. Major works will mean drawing up a plan of repairs that will cost thousands of pounds, and often be carried out on a whole block of flats or an entire estate in one go.

Sometimes major work of this nature will be supervised by outside firms of surveyors or architects, particularly if a large amount of rebuilding or internal remodelling is required. Larger organisations may have an in-house team to do this kind of work. In-house surveyors will work on identifying which properties should be included for a programme of major repairs. They are likely to work closely with the finance and development teams in getting the money approved to pay for the work.

They will certainly be a focal point for local residents who should get the chance of being involved with planning the work and choosing some of the improvements – such as the type of kitchen units and what colour front doors will be painted.

AIDS AND ADAPTATIONS

Most people prefer to remain in their own homes if they become disabled or infirm through old age or injury. Money is available to help with the cost of adapting homes so they remain convenient. It might be necessary to remove steps on a path and build a ramp, or install a lift, or in extreme cases build on an extra room for someone who needs to use a dialysis machine, or who can no longer sleep in an upstairs room. Assessing exactly what is needed is usually a job for an occupational therapist, who might be employed by the local council, or a hospital, or even by one of the larger landlords. Getting adaptations right is difficult, as so many parties are involved: the resident, perhaps their carer or family, the landlord, the council, the health service, the grant section of the council or even the planning department. But sometimes even minor alterations to the height of a bath or a loo, or installing some grab rails, can make the difference between staying at home or moving away. Surveyors will often be involved in this very time-consuming but satisfying work.

INSURANCE CLAIMS

All landlords will be covered by insurance for damage to their buildings. Some insurance claims are easy to deal with, such as when the wind blows a chimney off, or a tree falls and breaks a window. Most claims, though, are extremely complicated. A crack may appear in the wall of a house that might be due to the soil underneath expanding or contracting; or it might be that the property was badly built and has inadequate foundations.

The cause of damage is often unclear, so surveyors will have detailed discussions with the 'loss adjusters' at the insurance company, deciding what the cause of the problem is, what the cure is, and who is responsible for meeting the cost.

Skills and qualities

Surveyors will usually be qualified through the Royal Institution of Chartered Surveyors or through the Chartered Institute of Building. Many work for private companies, but most local authorities and housing associations employ at least some of their own surveyors directly.

Sometimes support will be given for trainees to qualify while they are at work, through day- or block-release.

The sorts of qualities needed in someone who will enjoy surveying are:

- a practical interest in how buildings are put together
- good diagnostic and analytical skills
- thorough and methodical ways of working
- coping with being outside in all weathers
- being able to communicate well with all sorts of people
- a desire to see things through to the very end
- ability to get work done through others.

Surveyors can't afford to be squeamish: much of their work is to do with drains and gutters and broken loos ... On the other hand good surveyors are worth their weight in gold, both to their employers and to the people who live in the homes they look after.

A day in the life of a maintenance surveyor

8am — Why does it always rain on Fridays? I'll just finish off that specification for the void property I inspected yesterday before I venture out.

9.30am — Can't put it off any longer. I'm meeting one of the housing officers to look at a flat where the tenant has been complaining of damp. Once inside we're quite shocked at how bad it is. There's black mould on the walls of her living room. I take readings, check the ventilation, look outside to see if there are any obvious leaking downpipes

---

or gutters. It's most probably bad condensation, but it's hard to be sure. We ask her about how she heats and airs the flat. You have to be very tactful, but she may not realise that sometimes the way you live affects the dampness in the property.

I promise to go and draw up a solution to the problem, but I warn her this may be just part of the answer. Dampness is notoriously hard to solve. The housing officer asks me whether I think the family should be moved out. The child has asthma apparently. We agree to try with fixed ventilation and making sure the place is heated properly, then think again.

10.30am A contractor's coming in to see me. There's been a real problem with tenants complaining his workmen don't turn up on time and are hard to communicate with. It turns out he's got a real problem finding skilled joiners and he's been taking on migrant workers. He says there's too much competition in the industry so he can't afford to pay his workmen much, but swears these guys are really good at what they do. He agrees to make sure that his office tells the men exactly where their appointments are and when, and gives them numbers to ring if there are any language problems on site.

11.30am Weekly voids meeting. We sit down with housing management and update them on all the repairs due on empty flats and when the target date is for the place to be ready for reletting. They blame our contractors for being slow, so we try and get early warning of when tenants are to move out. Trouble is you can't really tell what needs doing until the furniture has all gone and the flat is empty. The meetings are a laugh, usually, as we always try to see who gets their end of the work done quickest, us or the lettings team.

Lunch I go down the road for a sandwich, sharing an umbrella with one of the finance team who processes my contractors' payments. It'd help if we could get them done quicker. Small contractors are always on a knife edge with their cash flow.

2pm	Tender opening for the cyclical contract on one of our big estates. We have to follow very careful procedures to make sure there's no collusion on pricing. To my surprise, the lowest tenderer comes in within £1,000 of my estimate. I must be getting better. Or maybe it's luck.

All afternoon I clear my my emails, do my ring-backs, then get stuck into my monthly report for committee. I hear from one of the environmental health people at the council that they're going to give us a grant to put better sound insulation in between two of our flats in a converted house. That's great news.

Nice to get clear before the weekend for once. And we're all going down the pub later because someone's leaving. And it's stopped raining. It is my lucky day.

Chapter 4
TENANT INVOLVEMENT AND COMMUNITY DEVELOPMENT

TENANT INVOLVEMENT

There has been a major shift in the relationship between tenant and landlord over the last 20 years. As in the commercial sector, tenants are now viewed as 'customers'. Through paying their rent they are buying a standard of service and can influence the way in which that service is provided. Residents can now play a real part in helping set the standards to which the services they pay for are provided.

Tenants play a positive and constructive role in making sure work is done efficiently and well. There are different degrees of involvement:

Information

At the most basic level, there is a legal duty to make various kinds of information openly available to tenants. Most housing organisations will go well beyond this, by publicising their policies, practices and procedures through newsletters, annual reports, circulars, on their website, in local papers, on radio and so on. This is integral to good customer relations.

Consultation

Most tenants have a legal right through their tenancy agreement to be consulted about changes that affect them. Consultation might take place via a questionnaire, through an open meeting or by letter. For example, if a housing association decides to stop receiving rent payments at a local office, it will have to ask the tenants who use that facility what they think about the proposed change. The landlord will have to take into account what tenants say, but still has the right to decide to go ahead with the change.

Involvement

Involving tenants and local people implies a closer working relationship, perhaps through tenants' associations on estates. The tenants' association might work very closely with a landlord when, for example, major refurbishment work is being done on an estate. Tenants might be involved in planning the sequence of work, what kind of paint colours are chosen and what fixtures and fittings are selected. Public landlords work to fixed budgets, and tenants will often be asked to help prioritise where the money should be spent.

Tenants' associations will usually be concerned about their own estate's affairs, but more and more they take part in advisory panels, community groups and other bodies who look at the needs of the wider community and environmental issues which affect residents in other landlords' properties, private tenants and people who own their own homes. Some people will only want to be actively involved when they are bothered by a particular problem which affects their quality of life. Others may be interested in longer-term involvement with the landlord, influencing policy and practice in a wide range of housing-related matters. Social landlords are normally eager to include residents as much as possible and to offer training and advice to people who want to get involved.

Participation

While some residents only want to be asked about matters that affect them directly, others may want to make a wider impact. Boards or committees of housing associations will now usually have at least some tenant members. These may be elected by other tenants or they may put their own names forward. Each association is different.

Decision-making structures are changing, but local authorities will make sure that their 'Cabinet member for Housing' – the councillor who has overall responsibility for all aspects of housing policy in the authority's area – is well briefed about residents' views. In smaller districts where there are still housing committees, tenants' representatives may be co-opted in order to ensure that tenants have their views listened to and can play a genuine part in decision-making. In the LSVT associations, tenants may be in the lead. Many associations have tenants making up one-third of their committee membership. Committees will be responsible for policy and for deciding matters such as the level of annual rent increases.

Control

There are many ways in which tenants can take complete control of how their homes are managed. In a co-operative, for example, the management committee will be made up entirely of tenants, who will take all the decisions. Arm's-length management organisations, tenant management organisations and other new types of organisation put tenants at the front.

Community development

Many landlords now want to play a much wider part in helping the neighbourhoods they work in become better places to live. The changing industrial base of the country has led to economic decline in some regions. There is a higher proportion of unemployed and low-income households living in social rented housing than there is amongst the population as a whole.

A combination of factors can lead to the collapse of the local economy. Local authorities and housing associations may be the largest landlords in some of the more deprived communities and are well placed to use their resources for the wider benefit of the people who live in their homes. Residents may not have had the chance to develop their skills and capacities. Housing associations, for example, can make links with local schools, colleges and employers to create opportunities for local people, helping them into jobs.

Some social landlords are part of the Investors in Communities pilot programme. This is a national standard, like Charter Mark, which gives an award to social landlords who can demonstrate that they are working with their tenants in a coherent and collaborative way to improve their quality of life.

WHAT DO TENANT PARTICIPATION AND COMMUNITY DEVELOPMENT WORKERS DO?

Many large landlords now employ staff who work with local residents, enabling them to develop the skills and abilities they need to improve their own neighbourhoods. Tenant participation work will encourage people to get involved, setting up informal and formal tenants' networks.

Community development work means getting to know what people's concerns and problems are and helping them find ways to resolve those problems. The contacts and influence of the landlord can be very useful. For example, a tenants' association may be concerned about the lack of facilities for young people on their estate. The community development worker will work with them to identify what is wanted, might help with fund-raising and will help the tenants' group make the right connections. Arranging training for tenants is an increasingly important part of the work, equipping them with the skills they need, especially where they are involved in big regeneration projects.

Skills and qualities

Effective tenant participation workers will be good communicators who can encourage other people to develop their talents and abilities. They must want to enable people to do things for themselves. They have to be diplomatic and patient: real lasting change can take a long time to bring about.

A day in the life of a tenant participation worker

The trouble with my job is no one really understands what I do. Last night I was out late at a tenants' meeting on an estate. My employers want to see tenants' associations set up everywhere. The idea is great, but, to start with, people are either more concerned with other things going on in their lives or just suspicious. Last night, for instance, they were simply angry because there's a long-running saga about rotten window frames in the flats and that's all they wanted to talk about. Well, did they shout at me about it to start with! Still, everyone calmed down eventually and I can't blame them; from their point of view the windows must be number one priority.

But my aim is to help people to take charge of what goes on in their patch. This means helping them to organise themselves, unearthing talent, trying to encourage people to negotiate what's negotiable rather than just complain. Luckily I can take a long-term view. I used to work for a council that worked with its tenants and eventually had a vote to transfer all the properties into a new organisation which could release money for the repairs that were needed. Tenants took charge there in the long run but it took a while. I must be patient.

Anyway, I arranged with one of the women at the meeting that I'd pop down and see her today. She was too shy to speak up at the meeting. Went to her flat as arranged. She said there are a number of them who would like to get involved in something practical for the children on the estate. This sounds like a good way in to me. We talked about all the different sources of money available, from the Lottery to Europe. We think we're going to apply for a 'Community Training and Enabling Grant' from the Housing Corporation. Tenants might get training and skills for qualifications in childcare out of it.

I agree to get one of the community workers from the council to talk with her group about what the children might need. After a bit of nervousness she agrees that she'll put a proposal up to the next tenants' meeting if I'll help her rehearse what she has to say. She's interested in finding out about local courses now her children are both at school. She says her confidence is pretty low, having been at home with them as toddlers, and having left school with no qualifications. She seems really sparky to me, and I'll do whatever she thinks I can to help.

During the afternoon I'm writing a 'tenant participation strategy' to discuss with the tenant services director at my next supervision, when she goes through my work with me and we prioritise what I need to do next month. Especially important in a job like mine, which can be as big as I want it to be. She didn't think much of my first stab at it. But she helped me to understand what the shape of a committee paper ought to be, with recommendations and everything. We're looking at lots of different ways for people to get involved, from local events, through helping with our customer services training, to standing for election to our committee.

It's quite hard for some staff to get used to me putting the tenants' viewpoint all the time. But they are our customers and they know what goes on out there. We would do well to listen to what they tell us.

No evening meeting tonight but I'll go past the college and drop those brochures about courses off. Next time she can go herself, but it's hard to get someone to look after the kids when you're on your own with no money for babysitters and you don't like asking favours. If she takes up studying she'll soon be back to work herself, I'll bet.

Chapter 5
HOMELESSNESS

INTRODUCTION

Thousands of people become homeless every year. This may be because a private tenancy is brought to an end and they have no alternative place to go; it may be because a family splits up; it might be that domestic violence means children have to be housed elsewhere. In all parts of the country, especially London and the South East, there are refugees and asylum seekers who have arrived with nowhere to go.

Local authorities have new statutory duties under the Homelessness Act 2002. They must secure long-term accommodation for homeless people, working with other agencies. They have to compile a five-year strategy for tackling homelessness in their area. The emphasis is on prevention, on advising people who become homeless of how they can secure housing – and they must offer housing if children, older people or vulnerable people are involved.

Local authorities, especially in the big conurbations, will have teams set up just to help homeless families and individuals, where each person's case and prospects are carefully examined and solutions found. Sometimes, especially in the case of families with children, temporary accommodation in bed-and-breakfast hotels or hostels, paid for by the local authority, is the only answer, as the kind of permanent property the family needs may not be available immediately. Even in the more rural districts, homelessness is a serious concern, made worse by the fact that bed-and-breakfast hostels may be a long way away from where the children were at school or where friends and relatives live. And in the country, public transport for those without cars may be inadequate or non-existent.

Working with homeless families is extremely tough. The human predicament is hard to deal with when the kind of homes people want to live in are often just not available. This is particularly true in London and the South East, where housing is expensive and demand for it is intense.

Staff in homeless families teams will often have a difficult job establishing exactly what the applicant's history and entitlement is, especially if the applicant does not communicate easily in English. Staff will need to have good knowledge of the legislation and understand what applicants are entitled to. They will need to do a lot of liaison with other local authority departments, such as environmental health and social services. They will liaise with Government agencies and sometimes the police and probation service. Assessing applicants' cases is hard and takes time. Staff need to be thorough and patient, but meanwhile be able to cope with the frustration and anxieties of the person who has nowhere to go.

Working in homelessness is the true sharp end of housing. But it offers insights into the real importance of housing as a profession. It was the increase in awareness of homelessness in the 1960s that brought the pressure group Shelter to the fore, and Shelter, with others, promoted the growth of housing associations to help meet the urgent need for affordable housing.

Shelter

Campaigning, projects and housing aid and advice

Shelter offers:

Practical help

- over 50 Housing Aid Centres and Projects providing expert information, advice and advocacy to over 100,000 people a year in England and Scotland
- Shelterline, a free, national helpline providing advice and information 24 hours a day, 365 days a year
- five Homeless to Home Projects, piloting ways of resettling families who have experienced homelessness into new accommodation
- the Street Homelessness Project, working with local authorities and other voluntary organisations to develop local strategies for reducing rough sleeping
- the National Homelessness Advice Service, providing secondary advice to all Citizens Advice Bureaux

---

■ the new Homework Project, which seeks to prevent homelessness by providing information and education materials for young people in school.

Shelter also campaigns, and offers training

More information at www.shelter.org.uk

TEMPORARY ACCOMMODATION AND PRIVATE SECTOR LEASING

As bed-and-breakfast-type and hostel accommodation is not a satisfactory solution for homeless families, especially for the children, many alternative short-term solutions have been developed.

Some housing associations take leases on privately owned property for say three- or five-year terms and act as their managing agents. They then agree with the local authority to offer these flats on a furnished and temporary basis to families who are homeless and whose cases are being assessed. This is particularly useful for asylum seekers, where the assessment may take some time.

Managing temporary accommodation is a highly skilled job – the people housed are likely to be vulnerable and need a lot of support during this transitional period while they are waiting to hear what the final outcome of their application will be. At the same time the private landlord who owns the property wants to be sure that his or her property is well maintained, and that the rent will be paid promptly.

STREET HOMELESSNESS AND 'ROUGH SLEEPING'

One of the high-profile aspects of housing is the number of people who sleep on the street, either of necessity or by choice.

There are a number of voluntary organisations working with street homeless people. Night shelters and hostels offer respite. There are also organisations that specialise in helping 'resettle' people who have been used to sleeping rough.

Often finding someone a place to live is only part of the solution: people who have lived on the street may have other difficulties – health or drug or alcohol problems, no job prospects – or simply find it hard to adjust to the loneliness that a flat of your own can bring.

Young people who are homeless are particularly vulnerable, and organisations such as Centrepoint are there not just to help with housing but to enable young people to find training and work and develop the life skills they need in order to flourish independently.

Skills and qualities

As with housing management work, you'll have a real desire to help people who are going through traumatic times and often have intractable problems. You'll need to be resourceful. A combination of empathy, objectivity and energy will help you to help clients find solutions to their housing problems. And of course an understanding of the legislation and the work of other agencies who can help will be essential.

Chapter 6
OTHER KINDS OF ACCOMMODATION

KEY WORKERS AND STUDENT ACCOMMODATION

A growing market in rented and low-cost housing to buy exists among 'key workers' and students. Rental and home purchase prices in many areas, especially London and the South, have shot far beyond the means of people on low or average incomes. The Government has recognised the real housing problems of public sector workers, such as teachers, who although they have employment cannot afford to get on the house purchase ladder. To improve public services, it is essential to be able to recruit and retain good staff. The health service, schools, the police, the fire service and others all want to minimise the amount of travelling their staff have to do to get to work. Poor or expensive housing can add to the stress of working in a city like London, and these employers are keen to reduce staff turnover rates.

Nurses, for example, may need to live near their place of work, especially as they work anti-social hours, so cannot easily commute to places where housing is cheaper. Hospitals are transferring their staff accommodation to housing organisations who will modernise it and manage it to a high standard. Sometimes housing organisations act as managing agents. Or they may take a lease on the property or purchase it outright. There is now money being invested in housing associations to provide a range of homes for these key workers, both to buy and to rent.

The same sort of problems exist for students. Universities and colleges are transferring the management and sometimes the ownership of their student accommodation to professional managing bodies. Managing student housing is a discipline on its own. Instead of living in fully self-contained flats students are likely to have bed-sits where they share kitchens, common rooms and sometimes bathrooms with others. Students only need their housing during term time and are likely to go back home in the holidays. But the landlords need to have rent coming in all year round in order to be able to pay for repairs and renewals, and to repay the money they will have borrowed for the cost of building or refurbishing the accommodation.

This demands a different style of management from the other kinds of housing discussed in Chapters 1 and 2. But, as we have seen throughout this book, the skills and competencies you acquire if you start off running student housing will be transferable to other sectors, and just as valid if you decide you want to train for a professional qualification.

PRIVATE LANDLORDS

In the UK there are many people who rent their homes from a private landlord, or who own a long lease on their flat in a block the freehold of which is privately owned. The owners are mostly 'small landlords' – people who own just one or two properties that they rent out. Some are large institutional landlords, such as the Crown, the Church Commissioners and the old aristocratic estates such as Grosvenor, Cadogan and de Walden in London, which have large commercial as well as residential holdings.

There are plenty of opportunities in housing management positions here as well. The Association of Residential Management Agents and Association of Residential Letting Agents can give you information about the likely scope of jobs and what experience would be useful. The two main differences between private sector and public sector landlords are that the private sector landlord has more control over who to select to be a tenant and is unlikely to offer subsidised rents.

SHARED OWNERSHIP AND LEASEHOLD MANAGEMENT

In this sector too, changes abound. Where people own a long lease on flats in a house or blocks of flats, and a private landlord or company owns the freehold, someone has to be responsible for the painting and decoration of the shared parts of the property, such as the hall and stairways, and for repairs to roofs and lifts, and all contribute to the costs. Estate agents often manage these blocks on a contract basis. The legislation for leasehold management is changing and the style of management can be different from that in the public sector. Professional qualifications in this specific area of housing are being established. Joint management or service companies are being set up to do this work and there is a growing need for efficient operators in this expanding market.

Over the last 20 years many council and housing association flats and houses have been sold to sitting tenants under the 'right to buy' scheme. There are also a number of different arrangements that help people with low incomes onto the ladder of home ownership. Under 'shared ownership' schemes, residents buy a share of the value of their home and rent the remainder. This means the cost to them is somewhere between the cost of rent and the cost of a mortgage, and they have some equity in the property for when they sell up and move on. Mixed estates, with some owners, some 'shared' owners and some tenants, can make communities more sustainable and so are becoming much more common than the large estates of solely rented housing built in the past.

So landlords are often responsible for managing estates or individual properties where some residents are tenants and some own – or part-own – their homes.

Managing properties where residents have different responsibilities, rights and interests is particularly challenging. People who have a direct personal interest in the value of the property because they own it and may wish to sell their interest on are likely to be especially keen to see their home well maintained and the environment around it well kept. Friction can easily develop between neighbours who have different interests in how their properties are run, and people with a financial stake in their housing may have higher expectations of the service they get from their landlord – that is, the freehold owner of the property – than people who are renting.

Housing associations that offer shared ownership housing will also be involved in the marketing of new schemes for sale and the selling on of properties when owners move on. If the sales and estate agency side of housing appeals to you then you could get valuable experience in shared ownership.

Skills and qualities

As with the jobs described earlier you'll need to be super-efficient, well organised and able to cope with a demanding clientele. You'll find real transferability of your experience between the commercial world of estate agencies and private management agencies.

Chapter 7
CARE, SUPPORT, ADVICE AND BENEFIT WORK

Many tenants need care and support because of ill-health or other disadvantage. Many housing associations were set up specifically to work with groups who have special needs – not just for somewhere to live, but for help with running their daily lives.

These might include:

- elderly people who are physically or mentally frail
- people with mental ill-health
- young people who have grown up in institutional care
- people who use drugs or alcohol
- adults with learning difficulties.

The extent of specialist training and the qualifications needed by people wanting to work in care are beyond the scope of this book. However, it is worth being aware that councils and associations often work closely with voluntary organisations who specialise in the care and support of vulnerable people. Some councils and associations also employ care workers directly, especially those who work with elderly people who live in residential or 'care' homes, where 24-hour help, including meals, is provided.

If you are working as a carer in, say, a residential home, it is worth remembering that housing associations as well as local authorities may also have job offers available from time to time. A lot of people transfer from one sector to another. Hourly pay rates may not be very high, so other factors such as level of job satisfaction, journey to work, general terms and conditions (including training offered) may be things to think about especially carefully.

Some people moving into ordinary council or housing association properties who do not need full-time care do still have difficulties that are beyond the expertise of staff who are trained in housing management.

For example, they may have mental ill health, face language and cultural barriers or not be aware of the availability of both financial and social support. Although housing officers will always have some contact with social workers, the health services and the police and probation service, it is quite a specialist task to co-ordinate support for people who cannot otherwise live independently.

Associations and councils will often employ staff with special expertise to help vulnerable tenants to cope and to make sure that appropriate 'care packages' are in place and working. A new way of allocating money called 'Supporting People' has been introduced. This puts local councils in charge of deciding who will have priority for the money available to pay for help and support. There is a heavy emphasis on helping people to stay independent and live in their own homes for as long as possible. Securing enough help can present quite a challenge to housing workers, when tenants become more frail as they grow older.

Skills and qualities for working in care

You'll need to have a real empathy with your clients, who may be very frail; at the same time you need to be able not to get too personally involved. You must be practical and good at working with other people – teamwork matters a great deal in care. You need to have respect for all your clients, a desire to help them keep their independence as far as possible and an enthusiasm for training; a cheerful and patient outlook on life is likely to be appreciated.

BENEFITS ADVICE

The benefits system is extremely complicated and many people, particularly older people, do not claim all the benefits they are entitled to. As well as housing benefit and old age pensions there may be a range of disability entitlements that people don't know about, or think they are not eligible for. They may therefore be poorer than they need be, which affects their health and well-being. People whose work or family patterns change will find that the benefits they are entitled to change as well, and this may affect their ability to pay the rent.

There are many specialist positions in benefits advice, and much of the knowledge gained by people working in employment, social security or

Inland Revenue offices is transferable to advisory posts in housing organisations. The number of such specialist advice jobs available in housing organisations is small. It is more likely that you would start your career off in a Government department or at a council, perhaps administering housing benefit.

GENERAL ADVICE AND HOUSING AID WORK

Offices such as the Citizens Advice Bureaux receive a number of housing-based enquiries. Voluntary advice work with a CAB or independent advice centre can be a pathway into this kind of work, homelessness, housing advice and housing work generally. Some cities support the specialised work of independent aid and advice agencies that help individuals with their housing problems. This could include helping tenants facing eviction, or working with the environmental health department of the local council on health and safety matters, or countering the poor practice of a landlord.

The legislation and the regulations are immensely complicated and change frequently. Organisations that employ advisers, whether on benefits or on general housing problems, must be sure that thorough and regular training is given to ensure that advice is of the best possible quality.

Skills and qualities

You are likely to be good at this kind of work if you are interested in legal matters and the question of rights, accurate with figures, able to explain complicated things in a straightforward way to people who will not know all the jargon, and like to get things right. In general advice work you will find it useful to be a good networker and to have good knowledge of locally available resources for different clients, such as voluntary organisations or charities that can give help to special needs groups.

Chapter 8
LIVING ON THE JOB

CARETAKERS AND WARDENS

The Government is keen to see better management provided at neighbourhood level. Landlords often employ local estate managers, or neighbourhood wardens (or supercaretakers). Under the new neighbourhood management proposals these kinds of jobs will become more interesting and be invested with more authority and power to deal with problems on the ground. Landlords are now encouraged to work closely together with other organisations to improve the quality of life for residents. Neighbourhood wardens do not necessarily live in, but they might be tenants in the locality they look after. They will liaise closely with the community police, with youth groups and schools as well as the landlord they are employed by. They will have to deal with anti-social behaviour and will be involved with the police in combatting drug abuse and crime. They will build up good local networks and be in close contact with the housing staff. Often they act as the eyes and ears of the residents, keeping on top on any potential trouble spots and dealing with problems which arise on the street there and then.

Caretakers often live as tenants on the estate they look after. Their jobs may include a range of essential day-to-day practical functions, such as:

- keeping common halls and stairways clean and tidy
- changing light bulbs in communal lighting
- supervising gardening and grass-cutting
- sweeping paths
- ensuring that bin and park areas are well kept
- sometimes arranging repairs, or doing basic 'handyman' jobs as required
- keeping an eye out for any anti-social or criminal behaviour.

Usually caretakers will live rent free or with a reduced rent.

Caretakers and local estate managers play a vital role as far as tenants are concerned in keeping estates looking and feeling clean and well cared for.

The same goes for wardens in 'sheltered schemes'. These are blocks of flats or bungalows designed for people over retirement age, or people with disabilities, where a warden is available to offer basic help, as a good neighbour might, to people as they become more frail. Some sheltered schemes now use the cheaper option of linking into a 24-hour central call system – so that an elderly person can get help at any time – but wardens continue to offer a real service.

Modern Apprenticeships

You can earn money while working in a housing job by becoming a Modern Apprentice. If you want to go straight into a job, not study full time any more, this could help you get qualifications on the way. Details are available through your local Learning and Skills Council or Housing Potential UK (but see page 82).

HOSTEL STAFF, FOYERS AND SUPPORTED HOUSING

A number of councils and housing associations offer 'supported housing' to people who prefer not to or are unable to live alone. An example would be a house available for young people leaving local authority care or with learning difficulties who would need help learning to budget, shop, cook, clean, pay bills and so on.

Usually each resident would have their own bedroom and would share the kitchen and living room. Often there is a paid member of staff who lives in, and whose job is to help the residents with their day-to-day affairs. Sometimes these staff are employed directly by the landlord, but more often a specialist voluntary organisation will be responsible for deciding who moves into the house and who the house warden is. There are many different titles used for describing these positions – 'support worker', 'warden', 'hostel worker', 'support tenant', 'house-parent' and so on. There are also many 'floating support schemes' where the help goes with the individual (rather than the house where they live). 'Foyers' have been set up specially to offer young people training as well as housing, board and support.

If this sort of work appeals to you (whether living in or out), then it would be worth contacting the local or the national office of the relevant voluntary organisations. The National Council for Voluntary Organisations can give contact details. Here are some charities which have housing projects:

- Scope, which works with people with cerebral palsy
- Mencap, which works with people with learning difficulties
- RNIB (The Royal National Institute for the Blind)
- RNID (The Royal National Institute for Deaf People)
- Mind, which works to promote mental health
- Sense, which works with people who are sensorily impaired, usually through blindness and deafness
- The Abbeyfield societies, which provide for older single people who prefer not to live alone.

Addresses for these and other similar organisations are at the back of the book.

If you think you might be interested in a career working with people with support needs but are not sure, you might want to do some voluntary work first. Any of the above organisations can tell you what opportunities there are where you live. You may have a Volunteer Bureau or local Council for Voluntary Service near you.

Help the Aged, Age Concern and the Alzheimer's Society will be able to give you guidance about work opportunities with older people. Their addresses are at the back of the book.

Skills and qualities

Being practical, full of common sense and having a sense of humour are good qualities for caretakers and wardens, as much as for anyone involved in care. Empathy, a real desire to help other people, reliability and patience are all helpful qualities to have.

In care, training and qualifications will vary, but there is a wide range of qualifications available, and this might also be a useful background if you are thinking of moving into a career in social work eventually.

Chapter 9
OTHER KINDS OF WORK OPPORTUNITIES AND WORKING ABROAD

INTRODUCTION

All housing organisations employ staff who are trained in disciplines quite different from housing management, from accountancy to architecture. If you were aiming for a career in another discipline, it would still be worth thinking about the benefits of applying your technical and professional skills within the non-profit sector.

REGENERATION AND DEVELOPMENT

Much exciting work is being done to restore life to run-down areas. The 'New Deal for communities' programme is putting resources into many o the most disadvantaged places. Housing associations are involved in huge investment programmes, working side by side with major commercial investors. From Salford Docks to the Thames Gateway you will find housing development staff involved with planning how to put in new and attractive but affordable rented housing alongside the renovated industrial buildings and the shops and commercial centres. Websites such as www.thames-gateway.org.uk will give you a better idea of what is happening.

The larger housing associations have development teams whose job it is to purchase land for building new homes, to buy homes that need refurbishing or to work with other organisations such as local authorities on the large-scale regeneration of run-down central city areas. Often there are 'partnering' arrangements with major contractors, ensuring close involvement throughout the planning and preparation stage as well as when the properties are actually being built. Development teams will be responsible for seeing that the way in which land is bought and homes built ('procured') is strictly in accordance with all the guidelines laid down by the Government through the Housing Corporation in England.

As housing associations use a lot of public money for their work, what they do is strictly controlled. Costs have to be kept down, but the quality of what is built is very high. Associations have to be sure that their properties are of a decent space standard, and built to high standards of energy efficiency and sustainability. There is, however, much scope for innovation, using new materials and designs and finding ways of putting up homes more quickly by having the main components of the building produced elsewhere then assembled at the site. Not quite flat-pack housing yet, but new ways of producing homes more quickly and reliably are being encouraged throughout the building industry.

The development team will probably include people whose background is in surveying, architecture and administration. They will normally work with private firms of architects and private building contractors, and they will project-manage the whole building scheme – from the purchase of the land, through the design stage, planning and seeing the building work is done to timetable and to budget. It is worth remembering how varied the work of different associations is. Some work in rural areas, where there may be just as much challenge in building a handful of cottages in keeping with the long-established local style of building using local materials as there would be in putting up a new estate.

Smaller associations may 'contract out' their development work, using a larger association's staff to do it for them.

Development staff often enjoy good opportunities to move from one employer to another and will find their skills and experience as useful in a private development company as in a non-profit organisation.

Local authorities will often employ staff who have worked on the development side, to help make sure that housing associations on their patch make the most of the grants available to build new homes. These staff will make sure that planning applications meet local requirements. They may liaise with private developers, encouraging them to include some social rented homes in their new developments.

CASE STUDY

Joseph Ogbonna tells his own story

Born 1962 Studied to first degree level in Nigeria. Honours degree in Psychology (2.1) in 1984. Came to live in UK in 1991 with working experience of aptitude testing and construction project management.

Nov 1991 Worked for then Department of Environment as administrative assistant in the Housing Registry. Repossessions were rife and LSVT associations had recently been introduced. Registered and filed appeals from ordinary people to Government to intervene in individual repossession cases and local authority applications for consent passed through the Registry. They were interesting and I developed an interest in housing.

Aug 1992 Started training with PATH London (see below) and posted to the William Sutton Trust in Tring, Hertfordshire. Specific skills training and monitoring by PATH were crucial to job success. Placements within the William Sutton Trust included estates management positions in London and Hemel Hempstead, development, technical services, housing policy, allocations and lettings, finance. Exposure to various aspects of housing at an early stage enabled an understanding of my role and linkages between various services.

Aug 1993 First full-time position as housing officer (special needs) at London and Quadrant – achieved BTEC HNC (Housing) and Chartered Institute of Housing (CIH) Test of Professional Practice (TPP1) and started TPP2. Driven by a belief that career progress would be supported by a combination of experience and qualifications.

July 1995 Started six-month secondment to special needs development and progressed to permanent role as development officer. Completed CIH TPP2 module. Exposure to wide variety of own and colleagues' development schemes including general needs, special needs, student accommodation, health authority schemes.

Sept 1996 Started MBA (Executive) programme – hard work, being also employed and having a young family.

Feb 1997 Started employment with Octavia Hill Housing Trust as senior development officer, later senior project manager. Responsible for various new-build, refurbishment and major repairs schemes. Learnt valuable lessons in applying a customer focus to development and its impact on successful operation of a housing association. Timely for the introduction of Best Value in 1999. Completed MBA programme with emphasis on strategic management.

Feb 2000 Business improvement manager, responsible for initiatives to improve business processes and outputs including Best Value in Family Housing Association. Increased opportunities to utilise business training. Consolidating project management experience.

View that housing could provide a varied and rewarding career but progress requires hard work, investment in self-development and active management of own career. All this in an ever-changing environment.

PATH (Positive Action for Training in Housing)

PATH National is a skills development agency that aims to increase the employability and leadership qualities of black and ethnic minority people.

They offer two main programmes, for new entrants to the sector (traineeship programme) and for existing housing sector employees (fast-track management development programme).

For more information contact:
Research and Development Officer
PATH National Ltd
Whittington House
London N19 3JG
tel: 020 7281 8001
email: pranade@pathuk.co.uk

POLICY AND RESEARCH

Larger housing organisations, especially local authorities, need to spend a lot of time thinking about and planning how they will run their services to meet ever-changing needs and to help bring about continuous improvement. Research and analysis has become central to the way housing organisations operate, playing a real practical role in helping to find ways of doing things better.

All housing associations and councils have to keep very detailed records and statistics of everything they do and report to their own committees, councillors and also, ultimately, to the Government. These statistics, called 'performance indicators', help the managers and customers to judge how well they are performing compared with other similar landlords, and that means having to ask themselves whether a different way of working might deliver better results.

Public sector organisations want to get better at what they do. There are various methods and approaches to achieving 'continuous improvement'. Under a system known as best value, local authorities as public landlords have to compare both the quality and the cost of what they do and ask their customers what they think of the service too. So research, often through customer satisfaction surveys, interviews and focus groups, is vitally important and has a very direct and useful result. The emphasis is on finding better ways of doing things and on providing good value for money.

It is very useful for managers to look at their performance statistics regularly. This will highlight problems that arise, for example rent arrears starting to go up. This could indicate that there are difficulties with the local housing benefit office which need to be sorted out. Performance statistics might show that, while some repairs are always done on time, others are not, perhaps because a particular maintenance contractor is not working efficiently.

Sometimes the information presented in the statistics will cause a particular policy to be reviewed. In some parts of the country it has become difficult to find tenants for certain kinds of property. The statistics will show how long it takes to let vacant homes in different locations. If the statistics start to show that an estate or a street has begun to become undesirable, managers will need to see whether the 'lettings policy' for the area needs changing. For example, an estate might have a large number of families with children, but may not have good facilities for them. It may be necessary for the landlord both to work with the community to improve what's there for children and also to talk to the local council and get agreement to letting future vacancies to people without children.

Staff working in policy, research and information play a vital role in helping their organisation continue to meet housing needs in the most effective way. Staff will often be graduates, though not necessarily in a housing-related discipline. Research and policy skills are 'generic' in the sense that they can be applied to any subject – not just housing. Moreover, research jobs in local authorities and housing associations can lead to a wide varietiy of work for colleges and universities, independent research institutions, or trade associations such as the National Housing

Federation, professional bodies such as the Chartered Institute of Housing and for local or national government associations.

PUBLIC RELATIONS AND FUND-RAISING

'In business for neighbourhoods' is the new strapline for housing associations. 'Social' housing organisations have not always had a very good image – or, more likely, were not known about at all. Yet they have achieved an incredible amount in the 30 years since public grants were first made available for building more rented homes. Housing associations are dynamic and energetic and have helped millions of poorer people achieve a better quality of life. It is important that their work is known and understood, not just within their own communities but in the wider world. So the public relations side of housing has become very important.

Staff who work in public relations will have a range of jobs. They will be responsible for developing and improving relationships with the local media, with Members of Parliament and councillors and other influential people. They will probably be involved in developing the 'corporate identity' of the association – its logo and house-style for the website and printed material for example. At present, many associations are undergoing mergers and restructuring, and some go through the complicated process of changing their name and the image they project to the world outside. PR staff are likely to be responsible for publications, such as tenant newsletters, annual reports, and articles in the trade press, and for events such as the openings of new buildings, the annual general meeting, and staff conferences. Often they will be responsible for fund-raising for special activities. Making successful applications to grant-making trusts and the lottery is a highly skilled activity. Some associations have large charitable fund-raising teams who run everything from charity shops to sponsored bungee jumping. Some have old charitable endowments, the proceeds of which are used to support residents in ways for which public funds are often not available. These might range from small amounts to help residents purchase things they cannot afford themselves, or for the running costs of extra services which are useful to residents such as breakfast clubs for school children, through to huge sums for the building of new community halls.

Skills and qualities

People who enjoy public relations work are usually sociable and creative, with a good eye for detail and an awareness of the wider political context. They can usually write in a range of styles depending on the target audience and the purpose, for example journalistic flair for a tenants' newsletter, and a more polished approach for corporate brochures or annual reports.

MARKETING

While they often work together, housing associations also compete vigorously in all sorts of ways – for government money to build new homes, for local authority support for city regeneration projects, for contracts to provide care to vulnerable people and so on. Large associations will employ staff whose skills are in 'selling' what their organisation can do. This is highly competitive and is a growth area, with a fairly commercial approach. Many regions of the country have literally hundreds of associations. This number is set to fall, as money for new work is set to go to a reducing number of organisations, and of course no one wants to see their programmes cut. The marketing staff help explain to funders what special qualities their association can offer. This helps funders decide which will be the best association to work with on a particular scheme – ultimately who will get the work and the money to go with it.

Skills and qualities

Marketing staff tend to be confident and outgoing, good at presenting and getting their ideas across.

FINANCE

We have seen throughout this handbook how many of the skills needed for a career in housing can be transferred in from other industries. Nowhere is this more true than in the finance department. Finance departments think they are the hub of any organisation. In housing organisations they have the huge task of keeping control of and recording the money coming in – from rents, from government grants and from private loans.

Equally they keep control of the money going out – which will range from cheques for hundreds of thousands of pounds paid to contractors for building work, through salary payments, to handling the petty cash.

A large finance team will include people who are professionally qualified as accountants as well as those who are studying for management accountancy or bookkeeping and basic accounting qualifications.

The finance team will be involved in preparing the organisation's annual plan and budget, as well as forecasting financial viability for the next 5–15 years or more. Senior staff will be responsible for raising loans from private investors for new construction work and also obtaining approval for grants. They will do what is called 'treasury management', making sure that money is well invested. Because public money is used for building, it is very important that the financial affairs of local authorities and housing associations are run properly.

'Risk management' is a big part of the responsibility. This means making sure that no excessive risks are taken, especially on new schemes, that could damage the viability of the organisation.

Careful auditing is also very important, to make sure not just that the books are straight at the end of the year, but that good systems and controls over the flow of money are properly run, for the sake of efficiency and to minimise the risk of fraud. Annual audits are normally carried out by external firms of qualified auditors. The Housing Corporation regulates the full range of housing association work. The Audit Commission inspects local authorities and is now responsible for inspecting associations as well.

Calculating the annual rent charged for each property is a complicated task, as there are new controls and guidance from Government tending to keep rent increases down, while at the same time housing organisations must have enough money coming in to do repairs, repay loans, pay the staff and invest in new work.

Finance teams are always especially busy at the end of the financial year, when external auditors come in to check that all incomings and outgoings have been properly accounted for. Finance teams will be in charge of internal controls – making sure that there are proper procedures and authorities in place and enough cross-checking to prevent fraud or inefficiency in the running of the organisation's affairs.

Many finance staff will have the job of ensuring that money due comes in at the right time. This could include rent from tenants, government grants and payments due from local councils.

The rules and regulations and the way in which the accounts are presented for assocations differ from those in the private sector, but people who transfer in from working in private companies find it easy to learn which aspects of the work are different and which are essentially the same. Many Finance Directors and senior staff now employed in associations bring the benefit to their posts of previous experience in banking, or industry or commerce. Although the pay levels may be slightly lower, there are plenty of other rewards for working in housing. Some of these are described more fully in Chapter 11.

Skills and qualities

Good finance staff are likely to:

- be good at coping with routine
- enjoy seeing things through to the end
- be ordered and methodical in their approach to problem-solving
- be good at figure work.

INFORMATION TECHNOLOGY

Some exciting and innovative work is going on in using technology to improve services for tenants. Although this differs across the country, up to 50 per cent of tenants may have online access and there is great pressure from Government to modernise the way services are delivered. For example, experiments are being carried out by which tenants diagnose and report repairs online; tenants of some larger landlords can pay rent by swipe card; staff out on site can take laptops to help provide benefit and welfare advice; development teams bid for allocations of Government money online; annual returns are also dealt with electronically. Mobile phone technology is also being explored, especially as younger tenants are more likely to use a mobile phone than any other way of getting in touch. In local authorities, and most associations now, there will be an IT department that services the housing staff – carrying out upgrades, training and troubleshooting, developing new software for systems and so on. In small organisations the 'IT department' might be just one person, who will usually have learned the technical skills elsewhere. Hardware and software packages may be supplied by external contractors, in which case the IT people need to be very good at interpreting the jargon and translating what the housing staff want into language the techies can understand! The Government wants all services to be available online by 2005, so IT is a real growth area for careers in housing.

As with finance, IT skills are eminently transferable from jobs in other sectors.

Skills and qualities

In addition to obvious technical abilities, their good communication skills and calm approach to problem-solving make IT staff some of the most in demand of all.

HUMAN RESOURCES

Some housing organisations are now very big employers indeed, with upwards of 1,000 staff. Even those with only 20 or 30 staff are likely to need quite sophisticated knowledge of employment law. Housing organisations generally aim to be good and fair employers. Personnel teams – or 'human resources' as they are often called – will be responsible for:

- recruitment
- induction and training
- personal and career development at work
- restructuring (that is, implementing changes in the way people have to do their jobs)
- promotions
- salary and benefits packages
- union relations

- appraisal systems
- grievance and disciplinary problems.

Their work can be very challenging. For example, if one association merges with another, staff are likely to have to change their jobs, or may face redundancy. Incoming staff need to be helped to settle in with their new employer who may have different ways of doing things.

Continuous improvement is the watchword throughout the public service sector. Human resources staff will be closely involved in helping staff adapt to new processes and different ways of working, in spotting and nurturing talented people and helping people have satisfying career development. From time to time, they will be involved in the difficult matter of disciplinary procedures. They may need to help staff through a bad patch when health or domestic problems have affected the quality of the individual's work.

Skills and qualities

Staff in personnel are entrusted with all manner of confidences. They need to be fair and impartial, efficient at dealing with any problems that staff or managers may bring them (no matter how big or small) and genuinely interested in seeing managers and staff work harmoniously together. No organisation can flourish unless morale is good, and staff in the human resources field are crucial in promoting healthy and constructive relationships at work. Assistants in personnel departments may well train to become qualified through the Chartered Institute of Personnel and Development.

LEGAL SERVICES AND COMPANY SECRETARIAL WORK

Local authorities and some housing associations will have their own in-house legal teams. They may work on conveyancing of land or property, preparing contracts, helping with tenancy problems and so on. Company secretarial work in the larger housing organisations is particularly important. This is about making sure that the organisation always acts within its legal powers and that the way it is governed by its board follows best practice and is within its rules. There are increasing layers of regulation and inspection – not surprisingly, given the amount of public funds for which housing organisations are accountable. Solicitors employed within local government will be professionally qualified and may well have worked in private practice. Most associations appoint private firms to do their legal work. But as with all the jobs described in this chapter, legal skills are eminently transferable, and working for an organisation which has wider social objectives, not just commercial ones, may be very satisfying in career terms for those with a legal background.

OFFICE MANAGEMENT

There is one other area of work that is often overlooked but essential – office management. In any office a breakdown in the operation of day-to-day apparatus causes irritation at best – and meltdown at worst!

Office managers will ensure there is a continuous supply of stationery, that phones and faxes work well, that security is good, that the office cleaners do their work thoroughly, that the health and safety of employees is assured, that staff have what they need to do the job in the practical way of chairs, desks, files and so on.

Office management skills can easily be transferred from one kind of employer to another. Housing organisations often deal with stressed and poor 'customers', and having as welcoming and well-functioning an office environment as possible, within limited budgets, is important for both visitors and staff. So the office manager has a particularly interesting and challenging role. If the building from which the housing services are offered is in good order and works well, customers are likely to infer that the organisation itself is in good order and works well.

Skills and qualities

Office management jobs are often poorly regarded in terms of pay and status, and many people get their first work experience in a busy post room – don't throw this experience away: it could be useful if the practical side of making an office tick over well appeals to you. You see everything that goes on, and you will never be out of a job!

OTHER EMPLOYERS

If the general idea of working in housing appeals to you, but you want to get a broad understanding of the sector before committing yourself to a particular career, you might want to think about working in the Civil Service, the Housing Corporation (which allocates funds to and regulates housing associations) or one of the trade associations such as the National Housing Federation, or one of the tenant empowerment organisations such as the Tenant Participation Advisory Service. If you have a legal background you might feel drawn to the different ombudsman services that handle complaints from members of the public who believe their local authority or housing association has not dealt with their complaint adequately.

Inspection plays an important part in improving the quality of housing. The inspectors assess the performance of local authorities and housing associations and compare the quality and cost of what they do with their peers. The extent to which customers are really engaged in setting standards, and whether there is a real commitment to do better each year, is also assessed. Then the reports written by the inspectors on authorities and associations are made public. Authorities that prove themselves to be well run are rewarded with greater freedoms and opportunities. Those that do badly may, in the worst case, be taken over. Although the work of the inspectors and the regulators may be rather specialised, there is a need for applicants. The Audit Commission's Housing Inspectorate has inspectors based in its regional offices. Applicants from black and minority ethnic backgrounds are often in short supply for these posts. And the Housing Inspectorate advertises from time to time for inspectors who are tenants of councils or associations as part of the quality assurance side of inspection. Special training is made available for inspectors. An analytical mind, the ability to communicate well, an objective approach and an interest in improving public services would all be useful qualities in someone who wants to be an inspector.

Many new kinds of organisations are being created such as Housing Regeneration Companies and Urban Development Companies, all of which are potential employers for people with an interest in housing.

VOLUNTEERING AND BOARD MEMBERSHIP

Good governance (which means good leadership from the board which, like company directors, is ultimately responsible for how the organisation performs) is a really important ingredient for long-term success. At the moment, board members of housing associations give their time and expertise voluntarily, attending board meetings in their own time. It is likely that some associations will start to pay board members, in the same way that councillors and people who sit on the boards of health trusts can now be paid a certain amount for their contribution. One route to finding out more about what housing has to offer could be by serving for a while on the board of a housing association or as an independent member of an ALMO board. This might be particularly appropriate if you are someone who already has experience elsewhere, for example in a different profession, but are thinking of transferring into the sector. It is often hard to recruit board members, but people with a background in finance or business or IT, or in social services or health are in short supply. And if you are thinking of returning to work after a career break, this might be a way of easing you back in. The addresses and contact details at the back of this book may help you to find out more about the possibilities.

CASE STUDY

The story of a woman who came into housing as a mature entrant

Having spent a number of years in the 1980s as a single parent locked in the poverty trap of not being able to earn enough to pay for someone to look after my son while I worked, I grabbed the opportunity as soon as I was able to pursue my education as a mature student.

On leaving university with a qualification in business and finance I had a clear idea of the type of business I wanted to work in, but it wasn't until I began as a temp for a big housing association that I realised the varied career opportunities available in the housing sector.

I began inputting invoices, became the administrator for the HAMA Scheme (Housing Associations as Managing Agents) and have been the project coordinator for the information management and technology department for the past four years. I have been involved in numerous dynamic and exciting projects and now have an extensive skills base in project management.

Master of Business Administration, the MBA

Increasing numbers of people wanting careers as managers and directors in housing organisations are taking their MBAs. The disciplines learned in business administration are just as relevant and applicable to housing, where knowing how to plan and manage a business with a social purpose is, if anything, more complex than one driven by the need to satisfy shareholders alone. Some universities, such as Birmingham, offer courses that can be done part time alongside work; student Nadhia Hussain, quoted in *Inside Housing*, said, 'I hope to broaden my understanding of how different organisations work. The benefit of studying with individuals from other sectors, for example the police and the health service, is that I can learn more about the challenges facing these sectors in the 21st century. Learn to think outside the "housing box", if you like.'

WORKING ABROAD

Many other countries are building links with housing managers in the UK. For example there is an Asia Pacific Branch of the Chartered Institute of Housing in Hong Kong. Public sector housing work is widespread in countries within the Commonwealth, the EU, the USA and elsewhere, and there is a range of private sector agencies fulfilling a variety of management roles. In countries with a federal system of government, such as Australia and Canada, information about work opportunities is available from each state's federal government.

If you are thinking about working abroad in housing you would be well advised to contact the relevant Embassies or High Commissions of the countries that interest you to find out the opportunities and names and addresses of organisations which might help. The Chartered Institute of Housing will also be able to make suggestions.

Homeless International

This is a charity whose objectives are:

- to provide financial and technical support to charitable organisations and groups working to improve shelter conditions of the poor in Asia, Africa, Latin America, the Caribbean and Europe
- to support the international exchange of information and experience on homelessness.

Last year it worked in nine different countries, on 14 projects, affecting 1 million households, providing financial services, organising technical advice, acting as advocates, supporting partners and carrying out research into long-term solutions to poverty.

For more information check its website at www.homeless-international.org

Chapter 10
LOCAL AUTHORITIES, REGIONAL HOUSING BOARDS AND HOUSING STRATEGY

Although many councils have passed the management of their houses to other agencies, they have kept the most important responsibility of all – that of devising and implementing the housing strategy for their area. At the regional level, new boards are being set up to plan the investment priorities across the whole region. At the local level, there are now Local Strategic Partnerships which plan not just the housing, but the future infrastructure including employment and community development of an area. 'Enabling' is the word often used to describe a local authority's housing function. This means that the local authority has to work in partnership with other providers of housing such as private developers and housing associations, making sure that they provide homes which meet local needs. Local authorities have to make estimates of future housing needs to make sure that what is being built matches future demand. In addition, they have to

- have a strategy for tackling homelessness and have a system for helping people who become homeless and offering housing advice
- decide the best route to achieving the Decent Homes standard by 2010
- make sure that all homes, including privately owned ones, are in a good state of repair and that homes are energy-efficient
- tackle the problem of long-term empty buildings
- administer the waiting list for housing
- administer improvement and disabled facilities grants
- decide which housing associations to work with on which projects and make sure they spend the money allocated to them.

Some local authority housing departments have to maintain travellers' sites and mobile home parks. Some will have staff who specialise in 'green' issues. Staff may have a remit to help people meet their fuel bills.

Some will work closely with private landlords, encouraging them to provide housing for homeless people and others in need. Other staff may work purely on the policy development and research side and may be involved in the compilation and publication of performance statistics – all intended to improve the quality of what is achieved.The range of work is enormous and will reflect the particular history and priority attached to housing in the locality.

All authorities have had to review aspects of their work through a process known as Best Value. This involves working with service users to really question whether a service is as good as it could be, using the techniques 'Compare, challenge, consult and compete', commonly known as the four C's. If you go and work in any housing organisation, you will find some staff involved in this sort of review process.

Each housing department is arranged differently and will have slightly different responsibilities. But if you want a career in local government, the housing department will give you a fantastic insight into the real impact good local authorities can have on the quality of life of all their residents.

PART TWO: OTHER IMPORTANT FACTORS

Chapter 11
PAY AND PROSPECTS

Never has there been a more exciting time, with so much opportunity, to come into housing. There is massive growth, especially in the housing association sector, and employers want the right mix of skills to deliver new initiatives as well as maintain existing quality of service. Quite a challenge. It's a profession where individual staff can make a real impact early on in their careers. Rented housing in Britain is being transformed and neighbourhoods are being revitalised by all the investment taking place. There's a shortage of people coming into the sector, and a recruitment drive is under way to find people with the talent, energy and commitment to make a real difference to people's lives and to the prospects for their children. Employers now look for competency and potential in applicants, as much as for qualifications.

Housing organisations are great places to work, and some of the reasons are set out in this chapter. It would need a second book to give proper details of pay levels of all the different jobs in housing and how they are decided, and it would need updating every year. But there are annual surveys published that analyse the range of pay levels for jobs in different housing organisations, according to size and location, year by year.

PAY

Housing associations do not have jointly agreed pay rates for particular jobs. Each association will fix its own. However, they will be careful to look at what the market seems to be for particular positions every year, and keep an eye on what other similar employers pay. It's worth remembering that pay itself is only one part of what motivates people to go to work, and this is especially true for people in the housing world.

It's relatively secure work, as well as offering variety. Employers are likely to follow the best practice available when setting their policies for staff recruitment and retention.

As a big generalisation, in the urban areas, housing organisations are likely to pay towards the upper end of the range for jobs that are similar to those in the private sector – for example customer services and finance assistant jobs. Young graduates with a housing qualification and some experience working in central London might expect to earn around £20,000.

At more senior levels the position changes. The director of a housing department or chief executive of a housing association would probably earn less than someone with equivalent strategic, budgeting and staff responsibilities in the private sector. Obviously working in the public or voluntary sector means that people do not have the 'profit motive' driving what they do. The annual budget has to fit all sorts of externally driven standards, and the main source of income, rents, is controlled by government guidelines. Where salaries are essentially funded from rents and public grants, pay levels will not be exceptional, but they will take account of the market. But there are many other sources of satisfaction in this kind of work.

OTHER BENEFITS

Remember, when looking for a career it is very important to think about aspects of the 'benefit package', as it is sometimes called, not just the amount of pay in the bank at the end of the month in your first job.

'COFEM'

Career opportunities for people from ethnic minorities
In the North West a group of housing associations got together to look at ways of helping black and minority ethnic staff develop their careers in housing. This is part of their commitment to making sure that everyone has equal opportunity for personal and career development. They arrange secondments (where staff from one organisation go and work for a time in another organisation to widen their experience), mentoring (where young people get the chance to be guided and coached by experienced senior staff) and have a website with job, training and 'networking opportunities' – which means getting to know lots of other people working in housing and related jobs. This initiative has now spread to many other parts of the country. Latest information can be found at www.cofem.org.uk

Housing organisations are likely to be decent employers, with effective equal opportunities policies. They will probably offer pension contributions. They may pay for private health insurance – or at least for eye tests and screening. Paid annual holiday may be more generous than in the private sector, and, while paid overtime is not common, staff may be able to take time off in lieu of evening or weekend work.

Housing organisations are quite likely to be responsive to the needs of staff who take maternity leave or who have responsibility for caring for children or dependent relatives. Some of them have been in the forefront of 'family-friendly' policies, offering flexible working arrangements such as job-sharing or part time or flexi-time, some of which became new legal rights in 2003. Some are now using the opportunities offered by IT so their staff can work from home.

TRAINING AND PERSONAL DEVELOPMENT

Many housing organisations now have Investors in People accreditation, which means they take special care to train and develop their staff for the good of their business. It is usual for all staff to have at least an annual appraisal that will help identify their training and personal development needs and preferences for the future. Many organisations will offer regular in-house training and attendance at short courses and conferences. Some will let you 'job swap' to find out more about the different kinds of work available.

Larger organisations may offer in-house career development. You might for example start off as a receptionist, then move on to become a housing assistant, and be encouraged to study for a professional qualification with a view to promotion to housing officer when a vacancy comes up.

CASE STUDY

Dyane Kesto, London and Quadrant Housing Association Millennium Trainee

Dyane tells her story:

Well, my family and I left Wolverhampton, West Midlands for a fresh start in life. We heard that London had lots of job opportunities, while living in a town like Wolverhampton jobs were scarce. We moved to London in July 1999.

The first week of us moving I went to the Jobcentre and careers office to look for work. I finally found work with an agency. Two months after I started work I had a letter from London and Quadrant (L&Q) saying I had an interview. I was surprised because I didn't remember filling in a form for L&Q.

I went for the interview and realised when I got there that at the careers centre I had been told to fill in a form. 'This is a good one,' the lady in the centre had told me. She told me nothing about it so I just filled in the form.

The interview went OK because I got the post, and I was told it was for a Millennium Trainee. They told me what it involved, which was to complete an NVQ course, which I wasn't looking forward to.

But I soon realised that doing a course didn't have to be boring. I really enjoyed doing it, and I completed it too. I also got to work in other departments. The department I found the most exciting was customer services, where I was the first port of call for the tenants and each tenant had a different case. Some of them were nice and polite, others were not, which also helped me with personal skills I was lacking in.

This was a big part in my decision to stay with the trust. I enjoyed what I had learnt, wanted to better my skills, and I thought L&Q was the best place to better myself. Since working for the trust I have gained a great deal of confidence.

The most important thing that the training I had taught me is: we all know that we should put the customer first, and a good training programme tells you what that means – it shows you how.

An enormous range of support is available for staff who want to take professional qualifications while at work. Housing organisations may give paid day release or block release for approved courses, which might range in discipline from housing management to accountancy. Leave for study and exams may be granted, as may financial help for study materials such as books and journals.

Annual subscriptions may be paid for staff who are qualified in a relevant profession. Although you might have to agree to stay on for a year or two if your employer has supported you in getting a qualification, it is not at all uncommon to train yourself up with one employer and then move on to a more senior job elsewhere.

Summing up, then, public and voluntary bodies aim to offer pay and benefits to staff appropriate to the 'non-profit' sector. There will be no share options or big bonuses! But there are usually significant other benefits on offer – in addition to the prospect of job satisfaction and an enjoyable working environment. It's not a big world, and you tend to make good friends that you'll come across again and again as you move from job to job within the sector.

Above all, if you are at the start of your working life you should think about the enormous flexibility that starting off in housing will offer you. The next chapter looks at some of the relevant qualifications and other disciplines. If you find after a while that housing management is not up your street, you will be well positioned to change direction with good experience under your belt.

Chapter 12
PROFESSIONAL AND OTHER QUALIFICATIONS

Throughout this book we have seen that all sorts of different kinds of jobs contribute to organisations that provide and manage housing. Starting as a school-leaver, or as someone returning to work after a career break, is no barrier at all to promotion, career development and eventually taking a relevant professional qualification when you know what sort of work appeals to you and suits you best.

There are a large number of university courses in housing and in closely related disciplines. There are a growing number of courses in the wider subject of regeneration. A fantastically high proportion – more than 90 per cent – of graduates get jobs in housing within six months of completing a full-time degree or postgraduate course.

For the core discipline of managing property, qualifications approved by the Chartered Institute of Housing (CIH) are likely to be the most relevant.

What is the Chartered Institute of Housing?

This is the professional association for all those working, studying or with an interest in housing. Currently there are more than 17,500 members. It is a registered charity that exists to continually improve standards within the housing profession. As well as its role in education, the CIH runs conferences, training and events and produces publications and guidance. Its Good Practice Unit helps disseminate ideas and information, and its policy work helps shape Government thinking. The CIH has offices in England, Scotland, Wales, Northern Ireland and Hong Kong. There are active regional branches that run their own events and training. CIH members include housing officers, tenants, caretakers, repairs staff, housing academics, private sector landlords, board members and councillors with a wide range of positions and experience – all sharing a common interest in housing.

LEVEL 2 CERTIFICATE IN HOUSING

A level 2 Certificate in Housing course has been designed for people who have left school and who want to work towards either the National Certificate in Housing or the Professional Qualification, or who just want to have a better understanding of what housing is all about. It is a level 2 vocationally related qualification. There are four units to the course:

1. What is housing?
2. Communication skills for housing
3. Personal development for people in housing
4. Participating in housing.

To give you an idea of what this involves, the guidance from the CIH is that you have to complete all four units to get the certificate, and each unit requires probably 30 hours' learning.

Once the certificate has been achieved, you can choose to study other level 2 qualifications or you can go on to various NVQ level 3 opportunities. These include:

■ CIH National Certificate in Housing
■ other level 3 opportunities within housing-associated areas such as care
■ other level 3 opportunities outside housing.

The level 2 Certificate in Housing can also help if you want to gain Key Skills qualifications. There are three main Key Skills that are useful to have, whatever career you want to pursue:

■ Communication
■ Application of number
■ Information technology.

There are also three 'wider' Key Skills:

■ Working with others
■ Improving own learning and performance
■ Problem solving.

All of these Key Skills can be studied at four levels of increasing demand.

Property Housing and Facilities Management Skills

This is the new learning and skills council for housing, created through a merger in 2003 between Housing Potential UK and the national training organisations for property services. It is responsible for providing strategic guidance on education and training for people working in the rented housing sector. This is also the Standard Setting body for vocational qualifications. Housing Potential prepared a plan for Government to show what needs to be done to equip the workforce in housing with the expertise and training it needs to meet the constant changes and challenges of the work ahead. You can find out more about it through its website: www.housingpotential.com, where you will find:

- the new housing occupational standards
- Britain's largest database of searchable housing training containing over 1,000 courses from over 100 providers
- 'Training Together' – research into training across the housing care divide
- the housing sector workforce development plan – the basis for action and funding for staff development in housing organisations
- a range of news, research, features and reports covering good practice in the recruitment, retention and development of staff.

They are currently working on a project to produce an online career guide to help you decide the best way to both start a career in housing, and to develop it if you already work in the sector.

Try the Qualifications and Curriculum Authority too, at www.qca.org.uk

THE LEVEL 3 NATIONAL CERTIFICATE IN HOUSING

Once eligible, you might want to do further study in a particular housing topic. Topics include:

- Supported housing
- Tenant participation

- Housing management and maintenance
- Housing aid and advice
- Benefits.

You study six core units common to all areas of housing and six pathway units on specialised subjects.

Beyond that, there are higher certificates in specialised work such as student accommodation management. The certificates usually require you to complete four study modules, together with demonstrating what you have learned in your practical experience of the subject at work. The work is level 3 – A-level standard.

COURSES LEADING TO THE CIH PROFESSIONAL QUALIFICATION

If you decide you want to go on and study for the full professional qualification, there are a number of routes you might take. One is through taking the Higher National Certificate in Housing Studies (Edexcel) or the CIH Level 4 in Housing. This forms the first part of the CIH Professional Qualification and, like many other courses, can be studied by distance learning.

Study by distance learning is convenient for people who are already working or live a long way from the colleges offering housing courses. You are allocated a personal tutor and will also have to attend a limited number of day courses, but mostly you will be working from home. Check whether you live or work close to one of the educational establishments that offer relevant courses – there are 91 in the UK. To find out more you will need to contact the CIH Education Department on 024 7685 1776.

The academic part of the professional qualification is studied at undergraduate or postgraduate level. If you already have NVQ/SVQ level 4 you will be recognised as meeting the requirements of Stage 1 of the professional qualification. You can also reach it by completing the first part of an undergraduate award leading to a diploma or BSc/BA in Housing or the HNC or Level 4 Diploma in Housing.

The second stage of the CIH Professional Qualification is the professional diploma or BA/BSc in Housing. These courses are offered by a number of universities and colleges across the UK, and can also be taken by distance learning through the trade union Unison and through the CIH's own distance learning centre (dlc@cih.org).

Undergraduate and postgraduate courses in housing and related studies

Housing as a profession has no entry requirements as such, and you may get a job from which you can study part time, perhaps with support from your employer for day release, if you want to qualify. If you want to go on to study after leaving school but want to work as well, or are thinking about working part time while studying, there are related courses at universities and colleges all over the country, from Amersham to Ystrad Mynach! And 90 per cent of graduates get relevant jobs in the first six months. The CIH publishes a list of courses available, but it is a good idea to check with colleges direct for details.

If you have a first degree, and want to go on to do professional qualifications but work as well, there are ways to do both. At the University of Salford, for example, you can do an MSc, studying during year one from September till May, then doing a work placement in year two. This helps the employer by ensuring staff get full professional development and of course it is good for the staff, who will get better career opportunities through the qualifications they receive. And 30 per cent of those MSc students are in promoted posts within two years.

Some postgraduate courses are also recognised by the Institute as meeting Stage 1 and Stage 2 of the professional qualification. You might have to take a graduate conversion course if your first degree is not in a subject thought to be relevant.

Levels of the National Qualifications Framework	Housing Qualifications	Other Qualifications
Level 5	CIH Professional Qualification	Masters degrees Honours degrees
Level 4	CIH Level 4 Diploma in Housing CIH Level 4 Certificates in Housing NVQ/SVQ in Housing (Edexcel) BTEC Higher National Certificate in Housing	Early stages of undergraduate programmes
Level 3	CIH National Certificate in Housing NVQ/SVQ in Housing	GCE A-level Scottish Highers/Higher Still
Level 2	CIH Level 2 Certificate in Housing NVQ/SVQ in Housing	GCSE Scottish Standard Grades

Finally, to become eligible to be a full corporate member of the CIH, candidates have to complete a practice-based test called APEX, which demonstrates the candidate's practical understanding of housing service delivery.

While most professional members of the Institute become qualified by the processes described above, there is a fast track for people who are professionally qualified in other disciplines. So if you are reading this book because you are thinking about a career change, or you want to come into housing after a career break, you might already be qualified in one of these areas:

■ Association of Chartered Certified Accountants
■ Chartered Institute of Bankers (incorporating the Chartered Building Societies Institute)
■ Chartered Institute of Building
■ Chartered Institute of Environmental Health Officers
■ Chartered Institute of Management Accountants

- Chartered Institute of Personnel and Development
- Chartered Institute of Public Finance and Accountancy
- Incorporated Society of Valuers and Auctioneers
- Institute of Chartered Accountants
- Institute of Chartered Secretaries and Administrators
- Institute of Civil Engineers
- Institute of Legal Executives
- The Law Society
- Royal Environmental Health Institute of Scotland
- Royal Institute of British Architects
- Royal Institute of Chartered Surveyors
- Royal Town Planning Institute

or

- MBA/Diploma in Management Studies
- NVQ/SVQ level 5
- Three-year officer training course provided by the RAF
- Diploma in Social Work approved by the Central Council for Education and Training in Social Work (CCETSW)
- University of Leicester MA in the Management of Partnerships and Collaboration.

The CIH is also committed to the ongoing professional development of all those working in housing, so even once you are qualified, you are likely to go on expanding your knowledge and keeping up to date with the many legal and other changes which will happen during your working life in housing.

For more information contact:
The Chartered Institute of Housing (CIH)
Octavia House
Westwood Way
Coventry CV4 8JP
Tel: 024 7685 1700
Fax: 024 7669 5110
Email: customer.services@cih.org
Web: www.cih.org

Chapter 13
DIRECTORY

WHERE TO FIND OUT MORE

If you think you might be interested in finding out more about housing, there are a number of journals and magazines that carry information, articles and, crucially, job advertisements. Look at these carefully; they will give you up-to-date guidance about job prospects. Most housing organisations advertise widely and have a thorough process for assessing applications and carrying out interviews. They take equality of opportunity seriously and will make a fair assessment of the merits of all applications. Sending your CV in 'on spec' will probably not get you very far. Some specialised jobs may be recruited to through agencies. These are included in the addresses in the following section.

But, to start, try:

Careers Services Local services, both municipal and private or voluntary, will be listed in the local press or at public libraries, in schools or colleges. As well as advice, some services offer guidance on CV compilation, letter writing and jobsearch techniques.

Chartered Institute of Housing www.cih.org.

Council for Voluntary Services Local branch addresses can be found in the local press or in public libraries. Co-ordinates voluntary activities in the area. Voluntary work in the housing field is regarded as evidence of commitment as well as useful experience.

Guardian The Guardian newspaper on Wednesdays advertises jobs in housing, social care and related areas in a special supplement, 'Society'.

Inside Housing www.insidehousing.co.uk Weekly magazine for housing professionals – contains jobs section as well as useful news on current housing issues.

Opportunities, Opportunities, Link House, West Street, Poole, Dorset BH15 1LL, www.opportunities.co.uk Weekly newsletter specialising in employment opportunities in local government.

The Times, On Tuesdays *The Times* now published a supplement called Public Agenda which has job listings.

CENTRES OFFERING THE CIH LEVEL 3 NATIONAL CERTIFICATE IN HOUSING AND THE LEVEL 2 CERTIFICATE

North West

Furness College
Channelside,
Barrow-in-Furness,
Cumbria LA14 2PJ

Management and Maintenance
Sustainable Communities

Frank Cairns
Tel: 01229 825017
Fax: 01229 870694

Salford College
Worsley Campus,
Walkden Road, Worsley,
Manchester M28 7QD

Supported Housing
Management and Maintenance
Caretaking & Concierge
Services

Bernadette Hallett
Tel: 0161 211 5595
Fax: 0161 211 5060

Mid Cheshire College
Hartford Campus,
Northwich, Cheshire CW8 1LJ

Level Two

Judith Booth
Te: 01606 74444
Email: jbooth@
midchesh.ac.uk

Liverpool Community College
School of BTEC Studies,
Faculty of Business Studies,
Bankfield Site, Bankfield Road,
Liverpool L13 0BQ

Supported Housing
Management and Maintenance
Sustainable Communities

Frances Morriss
Tel: 0151 252 3839
Email: colcc@cybase.co.uk

Yorkshire and Humberside

Barnsley College
Old Mill Lane Site,
Church Street,
Barnsley S70 2AX

Supported Housing

Ruth Willaton
Tel: 01226 730191

Leeds, Park Lane College
Horsforth Centre,
Calverley Lane, Horsforth,
Leeds LS18 4RQ

Supported Housing
Management and Maintenance
Caretaking and Concierge
Services
Level 2 Certificate in Housing

Ian Taylor
Tel: 0113 216 2000
Fax: 0113 216 2020

North East

New College Durham Neville's Cross Centre, Durham DH1 4SY	Supported Housing Management and Maintenance	**Kevin Mochrie** Tel: 0191 375 4116 Email: kevin.mochrie@ newdur.ac.uk

West Midlands

Telford College Haybridge Road, Wellington, Telford TF1 2NP	Supported Housing Level 2 Certificate in Housing	**Wendy Bates** Tel: 01952 642237 Fax: 01952 642293
Matthew Boulton College Science Division, Sherlock Street, Birmingham B5 7DB	Management and Maintenance Caretaking and Concierge Services Level 2 Certificate	**Leigh Winfield** Tel: 0121 446 4545

East Midlands

Broxtowe College Arthur Mee Centre, Church Street, Stapleford, Nottingham NG9 8GA	Supported Housing Level 2 Certificate in Housing	**Ann Sare** Tel: 0115 917 5444 Fax: 0115 917 5445

Eastern

Suffolk College (University of East Anglia) Rope Walk, Ipswich IP4 1LT	Supported Housing	**Geoff Poole** Tel: 01473 255885 Fax: 01473 230054

London

Ealing, Hammersmith and West London College Gliddon Road, Barons Court, London W14 9BL	Management and Maintenance	**Mike Biddick** Tel: 020 8741 1688
Hackney Community College Brooke House, Kenninghall Road, London E5 8BP	Management and Maintenance Caretaking and Concierge Services	**John Lancaster** Tel: 020 7613 4951 Fax: 020 7613 9003
Lewisham College Tressilian Building, Lewisham Way, London SE4 1UT	Supported Housing Management and Maintenance Tenant Participation	**Jenny Rutter** Tel: 020 8692 0353 Fax: 020 8694 3349
CONEL/Middlesex University Bounds Green Road, London N11 2NQ	Supported Housing Tenant Participation Management and Maintenance Sustainable Communities Level 2 Certificate in Housing	**Geoff Ingarfield** Tel: 020 8411 4746 Fax: 020 8411 6282

West Thames College London Road, Isleworth, Middlesex TW7 4HS	Supported Housing	**Clifford Dixon**

South East

Mid-Kent College of H and FE The Horsted Campus, Maidstone Road, Chatham ME5 9UQ	Supported Housing Management and Maintenance Caretaking and Concierge Services	**Ray Fielder** Tel: 01634 830633 Fax: 01634 830224

South West

Bridgwater College Bath Road, Bridgwater TA6 4PZ	Supported Housing Tenant Participation	**Debbie Cummings** Tel: 01278 455464 Fax: 01278 444363

Wales

Barry College Colcot Road, Barry CF62 8YJ	Supported Housing Level 4 Certificate in Managing and Sheltered Housing	**Jane Wyatt** Tel: 01446 725000 Fax: 01446 732667
Pontypridd Technical College Ynys Terrace, Rhydfelin, Pontypridd CF37 5RN	Management and Maintenance	**Ian Lumsdaine** Tel: 01443 662800 Fax: 01443 663028

Northern Ireland

North Down and Ards Institute of F and HE Health and Social Care, Newtownards Campus, Victoria Avenue, Newtownards BT23 3ED	Supported Housing	**Carole Mowat** Tel: 028 9127 6600
Belfast Institute for Further abd Higher Education Department of Technology, Centre for Building and Civil Engineering, Millfield, Belfast BT1 1HS	Housing Management and Maintenance	**Michael Whittley** Tel: 028 9026 5423 Email: mwhittley@ belfastinstitute.ac.uk

Open Learning

Centre for Sheltered Housing Studies 1st Floor, Elgar House, Shrub Hill Road, Worcester WR4 9EE	Supported Housing Level 4 Certificate in Managing Supported and Sheltered Housing Caretaking and Concierge Services Sustainable Communities Call/Control Centre Operators	**Kate Roskilly** Tel: 01905 21155 Fax: 01905 22330

CIH Distance Learning

CIH Distance Learning Centre Octavia House, Westwood Way, Coventry CV4 8JP	All	**Philippa Russell** Tel: 024 7685 1789 Fax: 024 7669 4209

PROFESSIONAL QUALIFICATION – UNDERGRADUATE COURSES

England

North East

New College, Durham (www.new-dur.ac.uk)
Neville's Cross Centre, Darlington Road, Durham DH1 4SY

BTEC Higher National Certificate in Housing Studies (p/t)	PQ Stage 1	**Kevin Mochrie** Tel: 0191 375 4116

University of Northumbria at Newcastle (www.unn.ac.uk)
Northumberland Building, Northumberland Road, Newcastle-upon-tyne NE1 8ST

BTEC Higher National Certificate in Housing Studies (Management) (p/t)	PQ Stage 1	**Jamie Harding** Tel: 0191 227 4971
Diploma/BA (Hons) in Housing Studies (Management) (p/t)	PQ Stage 1 and 2	**Paul Grainger** Tel: 0191 227 4971
BA (Hons) in Housing (f/t)	PQ Stage 1 and 2	**Julie Clarke** Tel: 0191 227 4971

North West

Blackburn College (www.blackburn.ac.uk)
Feilden Street, Blackburn BB2 1HL

BTEC Higher National Certificate in Housing Studies (p/t)	PQ Stage 1	**Gail Barton** Tel: 01254 292337

Liverpool John Moores University (www.livjm.ac.uk)
Clarence Street, Liverpool L3 5UG

BTEC Higher National Certificate in Housing Studies (p/t)	PQ Stage 1	**Linda Wright** Tel: 0151 231 3629
Professional Diploma in Housing (p/t)	PQ Stage 2	**Linda Wright** Tel: 0151 231 3629
BA/BA (Hons) Housing Studies (p/t)	PQ Stage 1 and 2	**Linda Wright** Tel: 0151 231 3629
BA (Hons) Housing Studies (f/t)	PQ Stage 1 and 2. No sandwich element.	**Linda Wright** Tel: 0151 231 3629

University of Salford (www.salford.ac.uk)
Allerton Building, Frederick Road, Salford M6 6PU

BTEC Higher National Certificate in Housing Studies (p/t)	PQ Stage 1	**Julia Lucas** Tel: 0161 295 2177

Diploma in Higher Education in Housing Studies (p/t)		**Julia Lucas** Tel: 0161 295 2177
BSc (Hons) Housing Studies (p/t)	PQ Stage 1 and 2	**John Shenton** Tel: 0161 295 2193
BSc (Hons) Housing Studies (f/t)	PQ Stage 1 and 2	**John Shenton** Tel: 0161 295 2193

Yorkshire and Humberside

Leeds Metropolitan University (www.lmu.ac.uk)
Brunswick Building, Leeds LS2 8BU

Foundation Degree in Housing (p/t)	PQ Stage 1 and 2. With Park Lane College	**Ed Whalley** Tel: 0113 283 2600
Diploma in Higher Education/BA (Hons) in Housing Studies (p/t)	PQ Stage 2	**Jane Kettle** Tel: 0113 283 2600

Park Lane College, Leeds (www.parklanecoll.ac.uk)
Horsforth Centre, Calverley Lane, Horsforth, Leeds LS7 4HB

BTEC Higher National Certificate in Housing Studies (p/t)	PQ Stage 1	**Ian Taylor** Tel: 0116 216 2320
Foundation Degree in Housing (p/t)	PQ Stage 1 and 2. With Leeds Met University	**Christine Tordoff** Tel: 0116 216 2320

Sheffield Hallam University (www.shu.ac.uk)
City Campus, Howard Street, Sheffield S1 1WB

BTEC Higher National Certificate in Housing Studies (p/t)	PQ Stage 1	**Glen Gidley** Tel: 0114 225 4004
Professional Diploma in Housing (p/t)	PQ Stage 2	**Colin Foster** Tel: 0114 225 3538
BA (Hons) Housing Studies (p/t)	PQ Stage 1 and 2	**Steve Hills** Tel: 0114 225 2819
BA (Hons) Housing Studies (f/t)	PQ Stage 1 and 2. 4-year sandwich course	**Steve Hills** Tel: 0114 285 2819

Wakefield College (www.wakcoll.ac.uk)
Thornes Park Campus, Thornes Park, Wakefield WF1 2DH

BTEC Higher National Certificate in Housing Studies (p/t)	PQ Stage 1	**Lorraine Schofield** Tel: 01977 554571

Doncaster College (www.don.ac.uk)
Waterdale, Doncaster DN1 3EX

BTEC Higher National Certificate in Housing Studies (p/t)	PQ Stage 1	**Ayuba Lawan** Tel: 01302 553553

West Midlands

University of Central England, Birmingham (www.uce.ac.uk)
Perry Barr, Birmingham B42 2SU

BTEC Higher National Certificate in Housing Studies (p/t)	PQ Stage 1	**Naomi Faulkner** Tel: 0121 331 5116
BA Professional Housing Studies (p/t)	PQ Stage 1 and 2	**Naomi Faulkner** Tel: 0121 331 5116
BA (Hons) Housing (f/t)	PQ Stage 1 and 2. No sandwich element	**Naomi Faulkner** Tel: 0121 331 5116

Stoke-on-Trent College (www.stokecoll.ac.uk)
Burslem Campus, Moorland Road, Burslem, Stoke-on-Trent ST6 1JJ

BTEC Higher National Certificate in Housing Studies (p/t)	PQ Stage 1	**Fred Oakden** Tel: 01782 208208

Worcester College of Technology (www.wortech.ac.uk)
Deansway, Worcester WR1 2JF

BTEC Higher National Certificate in Housing Studies (p/t)	PQ Stage 1	**Bryn Griffiths** Tel: 01905 725616

East Midlands

De Montfort University, Leicester (www.dmu.ac.uk)
The Gateway, Leicester LE1 9BH

BTEC Higher National Certificate in Housing Studies (p/t)	PQ Stage 1	**Liz Millward** Tel: 0116 255 1551
BSc/BSc (Hons) in Housing Studies (p/t)	PQ Stage 1 and 2	**Liz Millward** Tel: 0116 255 1551

Stephenson College, Coalville (www.stephensoncoll.ac.uk)
Bridge Road, Coalville LE67 2PN

BTEC Higher National Certificate in Housing Studies (p/t)	PQ Stage 1	Tel: 01530 836136

Eastern

Anglia Polytechnic University (www.anglia.ac.uk)
Bishop Hall Lane, Chelmsford CM1 1SQ

Diploma in Housing (p/t)	PQ Stage 1 and 2	**Martin Dean** Tel: 01245 493131
BSc (Hons) Housing (f/t)	PQ Stage 1 and 2. 3 or 4 year (w/sandwich) course	**Martin Dean** Tel: 01245 493131

City College, Norwich (www.ccn.ac.uk)
Ipswich Road, Norwich NR2 2LJ

BTEC Higher National Certificate in Housing Studies (p/t)	PQ Stage 1	**Claire Collen** Tel: 01603 773282

London

University of Greenwich (www.gre.ac.uk)
Avery Hill Campus, Avery Hill Road, London SE9 2UG

Diploma of Higher Education in Housing Studies (p/t)	PQ Stage 2	**Maureen Rhoden** Tel: 020 8331 9300
BSc (Hons) Housing Studies (p/t)	Top-up from Diploma	**Maureen Rhoden** Tel: 020 8331 9300
BSc (Hons) Housing Studies (f/t)	PQ Stage 1 and 2	**Maureen Rhoden** Tel: 020 8331 9300

The Community College, Hackney (www.comm-coll-hackney.ac.uk)
Brooke House, Kenninghall Road, London E5 8BP

BTEC Higher National Certificate in Housing Studies (p/t)	PQ Stage 1	**John Lancaster** Tel: 020 7613 9417

Ealing, Hammersmith & West London College (www.hwlc.ac.uk)
Gliddon Road, Barons Court, London W14 9BL

BTEC Higher National Certificate in Housing Studies (p/t)	PQ Stage 1	**Charlotte Harris** Tel: 020 8741 1688

CONEL/Middlesex University (www.conel.ac.uk/www.mdx.ac.uk)
Bounds Green Campus, Bounds Green Road, London N11 2NQ

Foundation Degree in Housing (p/t)	PQ Stage 1 and 2	**Geoff Ingarfield** Tel: 020 8802 3111
BSc (Hons) Housing Studies (p/t)	PQ Stage 1 and 2	**Patrick Mulrenan** Tel: 020 8362 5188
BSc (Hons) Housing Studies (f/t)	PQ Stage 1 and 2	**Patrick Mulrenan** Tel: 020 8362 5188

College of North West London (www.cnwl.ac.uk)
Willesden Centre, Dudden Hill Lane, London NW10 2XD

BTEC Higher National Certificate in Housing Studies (p/t)	PQ Stage 1	**Robert Mather** Tel: 020 8208 5000

South Bank University (www.sbu.ac.uk)
Wandsworth Road, London SW8 2JZ

BTEC Higher National Certificate in Housing Studies (p/t)	PQ Stage 1	**Alan Winter** Tel: 020 7815 7170

BA/BA (Hons) Housing Studies (p/t)	PQ Stage 1 and 2	**Alan Winter** Tel: 020 7815 7170

University of Westminster (www.wmin.ac.uk)
35 Marylebone Road, London NW1 5LS

Diploma/BA (Hons) Housing Management & Development (p/t)	PQ Stage 1 and 2	**Anna Haworth** Tel: 020 7911 5000
BA (Hons) Housing Management & Development (f/t)	PQ Stage 1 and 2. 3 or 4 year (w/sandwich) course	**Tony Manzi** Tel: 020 7911 5000

South East

Mid-Kent College of Higher & Further Education (www.midkent.ac.uk)
Horsted Centre, Maidstone Road, Chatham ME5 9UQ

BTEC Higher National Certificate in Housing Studies (p/t)	PQ Stage 1	**Geoff Rose** Tel: 01634 830633

North East Surrey College of Technology (NESCOT) (www.nescot.ac.uk)
Reigate Road, Ewell, Epsom KT17 3DS

BTEC Higher National Certificate in Housing Studies (p/t)	PQ Stage 1	**Roger Jennings** Tel: 020 8394 3193
Professional Diploma in Housing (p/t)	PQ Stage 2	**Roger Jennings** Tel: 020 8394 3193

Southampton Institute (www.solent.ac.uk)
East Park Terrace, Southampton SO14 0YN

BTEC Higher National Certificate in Housing Studies (p/t)	PQ Stage 1	**Gill Tunney** Tel: 023 8031 9026
Professional Diploma in Housing (p/t)	PQ Stage 2	Tel: 023 8031 9026

South West

Bridgwater College (www.bridgwater.ac.uk)
Bath Road, Bridgwater TA6 4PZ

BTEC Higher National Certificate in Housing Studies (p/t)	PQ Stage 1	**Jane Hilton** Tel: 01278 455464

City of Bristol College (www.cityofbristol.ac.uk)
Downend Centre, Beaufort Road, Downend, Bristol BS16 6UH

BTEC Higher National Certificate in Housing Studies (p/t)	PQ Stage 1	**Derek Brewer** Tel: 0117 904 5000

University of the West of England, Bristol (www.uwe.ac.uk)
Coldharbour Lane, Frenchay, Bristol BS16 1QY

Diploma in Housing & Development (p/t)	PQ Stage 2	**Judith Ritchie** Tel: 0117 965 6261

BA (Hons) Housing & Development (p/t)	PQ Stage 1 and 2	**Judith Ritchie** Tel: 0117 965 6261
BA (Hons) Housing Studies (f/t)	PQ Stage 1 and 2. Sandwich course	**Judith Ritchie** Tel: 0117 965 6261

Swindon College (www.swindon-college.ac.uk)
Regent Circus, Swindon SN1 1PT

BTEC Higher National Certificate in Housing Studies (p/t)	PQ Stage 1	**Jim Hall** Tel: 01793 491915

Wales

North East Wales Institute of Higher Education (www.newi.ac.uk)
Plas Coch, Mold Road, Wrexham LL11 2AW

BTEC Higher National Certificate in Housing Studies (p/t)	PQ Stage 1	**Jon Talbot** Tel: 01978 293281
Diploma in Higher Education in Housing (p/t)	PQ Stage 2	**Jane Wafer** Tel: 01978 293098
BSc/BSc (Hons) in Housing (p/t)	Top-up from Diploma	**Jane Wafer** Tel: 01978 293098
BSc (Hons) in Housing (f/t)	PQ Stage 1 and 2	**Jane Wafer** Tel: 01978 293098

University of Wales Institute, Cardiff (www.uwic.ac.uk)
Llandaff Campus, Western Avenue, Cardiff CF5 2YB

BTEC Higher National Certificate in Housing Studies (p/t)	PQ Stage 1	**Nigel Rees** Tel: 029 2050 6823
UWIC Diploma in Higher Education in Housing Studies (p/t)	PQ Stage 2	**Sue Finch** Tel: 029 2050 6823
BSc/BSc (Hons) Housing Studies (p/t)	PQ Stage 1 and 2	**Sue Finch** Tel: 029 2050 6823
BSc (Hons) Housing Studies (f/t)	PQ Stage 1 and 2	**Sue Finch** Tel: 029 2050 6823

Scotland

Aberdeen College (www.abcol.ac.uk)
Gallowgate Centre, Gallowgate, Aberdeen AB25 1DN

SQA Higher National Certificate in Housing Studies (p/t)	PQ Stage 1	**Myra Calder** Tel: 01224 612033

Dundee College of Further Education (www.dundeecoll.ac.uk)
Constitution Campus, 30 Constitution Road, Dundee DD3 6TB

SQA Higher National Certificate in Housing Studies (p/t)	PQ Stage 1	**David McAllister** Tel: 01382 834834

Edinburgh's Telford College (www.ed-coll.ac.uk)
Crewe Toll, Edinburgh EH4 2NZ

SQA Higher National Certificate in Housing Studies (p/t)	PQ Stage 1	**Alan Smith** Tel: 0131 332 2491

Glasgow College of Building & Printing (www.gcbp.ac.uk)
60 North Hanover Street, Glasgow G1 2BP

SQA Higher National Certificate in Housing Studies (p/t)	PQ Stage 1	**Anne Murphy** Tel: 0141 332 9969

Kilmarnock College (www.kilmarnock.ac.uk)
Holehouse Road, Kilmarnock KA3 7AT

SQA Higher National Certificate in Housing Studies (p/t)	PQ Stage 1	**Tesfaye Eshetu** Tel: 01563 523501

Motherwell College (www.motherwell.ac.uk)
Dalzell Drive, Motherwell ML4 2DD

SQA Higher National Certificate in Housing Studies (p/t)	PQ Stage 1	**Jean Murphy** Tel: 01698 232222

Northern Ireland

University of Ulster (www.ulst.ac.uk)
Magee Campus, Northland Road, Londonderry BT48 7JL

BSc (Hons) Housing Policy and Management (f/t)	PQ Stage 1 and 2. 4 year (w/sandwich) course	**Patrick Gray** Tel: 028 7137 1371

Distance Learning

Chartered Institute of Housing Distance Learning Centre (www.cih.org)
Octavia House, Westwood Way, Coventry CV4 8JP

BTEC Higher National Certificate in Housing Studies (p/t)	PQ Stage 1	**Vicky Serpell** Tel: 024 7685 1789
CIH Professional Diploma in Housing Studies (p/t)	PQ Stage 2	**Vicky Serpell** Tel: 024 7685 1789

UNISON Open College (www.unison-opencollege.org)
1 Mabledon Place, London WC1H 9AJ

Professional Diploma in Housing (p/t)	PQ Stage 2	**Sandra Hann** Tel: 020 7388 2366

USEFUL ADDRESSES

Abbeyfield Society
Abbeyfield House
53 Victoria Street
St Albans
Herts AL1 3UW
Tel: 01727 857 536
Fax: 01727 846 168
Email: enquiries@abbeyfield.com

Age Concern (Cymru)
4th Floor
1 Cathedral Road
Cardiff CF11 9SD
Tel: 029 2037 1566
Fax: 029 2039 9562
Email: enquiries@accymru.org.uk
Web: www.accymru.org.uk

Age Concern (England)
Astral House
1268 London Road
London SW16 4ER
Tel: 020 8679 8000
Fax: 020 8679 6069
Email: ace@ace.org.uk
Web: www.ace.org.uk

Age Concern (Northern Ireland)
3 Lower Crescent
Belfast BT7 1NR
Tel: 028 9024 5729
Email: ageconcern.ni@btinternet.com

Age Concern (Scotland)
113 Rose Street
Edinburgh EH2 3DT
Tel: 0131 220 3345

Fax: 0131 220 2779
Email: enquiries@
acsinfo3.freeserve.co.uk

Alzheimer's Society
Gordon House
10 Greencoat Place
London SW1P 1PH
Tel: 020 7306 0606
Fax: 020 7306 0808
Email: info@alzheimers.org.uk
Web: www.alzheimers.org.uk

Association of Residential Letting
Agents (ARLA)
Maple House
53–55 Woodside Road
Amersham
Bucks HP6 6AA
Tel: 0845 345 5752
Fax: 01494 431530
Email: info@arla.co.uk

Association of Residential
Management Agents
178 Battersea Park Road
London SW11 4ND
Tel: 020 7978 2607
Fax: 020 7498 6153
Email: info@arma.org.uk
Web: www.arma.org.uk

Association of Retirement Housing
Managers
3rd Floor
Albert Embankment
London SE1 7TP

Tel and Fax: 020 7820 1839
Email: enquiries@arhm.org
Web: www.arhm.org

Audit Commission
1 Vincent Square
London SW1P 2PN
Tel: 020 7828 1212
Fax: 020 7976 6187
Email: enquiries@audit-commission.
gov.uk
Web: www.audit-commission.gov.uk/

Audit Commission in Wales
4th Floor
Deri House
2–4 Park Grove
Cardiff CF10 3ZZ
Tel: 029 2026 2550
Fax: 029 2039 7070
Web: www.audit-commission. gov.uk/

Audit Scotland
110 George Street
Edinburgh EH2 4LH
Tel: 0131 477 1234
Fax: 0131 477 4567
Email: info@audit-scot.gov.uk
Web: www.audit-scotland.gov.uk.

Building Societies Association
3 Savile Row
London W1S 3PB
Tel: 020 7437 0655
Fax: 020 7734 6416
Email: name@bsa.org.uk
Web: www.bsa.org.uk/

Care and Repair England
3rd Floor, Bridgford House
Pavilion Road
West Bridgford
Nottingham NG2 5GJ
Tel: 0115 982 1527
Fax: 0115 982 1529

Email: info@careandrepair-england.
org.uk
Web: www.careandrepair-england.
org.uk/

Care and Repair Cymru
Norbury House
Norbury Road
Fairwater
Cardiff CF5 3AS
Tel: 029 2057 6286
Fax: 029 2057 6283
Web: www.careandrepair.org.uk

Catholic Housing Aid Society
209 Old Marylebone Road
London NW1 5QT
Tel: 020 7723 7273
Fax: 020 7723 5943
Email: info@chasnational.org.uk
Web: www.chasnational.org.uk

CECODHAS (European Liaison
Committee for Social Housing)
Executive Secretary
Tineke Zuidervaart
Aedes, Hilversum,
Olympia 1
NL-1213 NS Hilversum
The Netherlands
Tel: (+) 31 35 626 83 33
Fax: (+) 31 35 626 84 33
Email: ir@aedesnet.nl
Web: www.cecodhas.org

Representative in Brussels
Claire Roumet
40 Rue des Colonies
B-1000 Bruxelles
Belgium
Tel: (+) 32 2 505 45 00
Fax: (+) 32 2 505 44 99
Email: cecodhas@vhm.be

Centre for Housing Management and
Development
College of Cardiff
University of Wales
Dept of City and Regional Planning
PO Box 906
Cardiff CF1 3YN
Tel: 029 2087 4000
Fax: 029 2087 4845
Web: www.cardiff.ac.uk

Centre for Housing Policy
University of York
Heslington
York YO10 5DD
Tel: 01904 433691
Fax: 01904 432318
Email: mj12@york.ac.uk
Web: www.york.ac.uk/inst/chp/

Centre for Regional Economic and
Social Research
School of Environment and
Development
Sheffield Hallam University
City Campus
Sheffield S1 1WB
Tel: 0114 225 4267
Fax: 0114 225 3179
Email: sed@shu.ac.uk
Web: www.shu.ac.uk/cresr/ for
Regional Economic and Social
Research

Centre for Urban and Regional Studies
J G Smith Building
The University of Birmingham
Edgbaston
Birmingham B15 2TT
General Enquiries:
Tel: 0121 414 5021
Fax: 0121 414 3279
Email: name@bham.ac.uk
Web: www.spp3.bham.ac.uk/curs/

Centrepoint
Neil House
7 Whitechapel Road
London E1 1DU
Tel: 020 7426 5300
Fax: 020 7426 5301
Email: name@centrepoint.org.uk
Web: www.centrepoint.org.uk

Chartered Institute of Building
Englemere
Kings Ride
Ascot
Berks SL5 7TB
Tel: 01344 630700
Fax: 01344 630777
Email: reception@ciob.org.uk
Web: www.ciob.org.uk

Chartered Institute of Environmental
Health
Chadwick Court
15 Hatfields
London SE1 8DJ
Tel: 020 7928 6006
Fax: 020 7827 5866
Email: cieh@cieh.org
Web: www.cieh.org.uk/

Chartered Institute of Housing (CIH)
Headquarters
Octavia House
Westwood Way
Coventry CV4 8JP
Tel: 024 7685 1700
Fax: 024 7669 5110
Email: customer.services@cih.org
Web: www.cih.org

CIH Cymru
Tel: 029 2076 5760
Fax: 029 2076 5761
Email: cymru@cih.org and
cymru.training@cih.org

CIH in Northern Ireland
Tel: 028 9077 8222
Fax: 028 9077 8333
Email: ni@cih.org and
ni.training@cih.org

CIH in Scotland
Tel: 0131 225 4544
Fax: 0131 225 4566
Email: scotland@cih.org and
scotland.training@cih.org

CIH London Office
Tel: 020 7837 4280
Fax: 020 7278 2705
Email: london@cih.org and
press@cih.org

CIH Asia Pacific
Tel: (00) 852 2356 8680
Fax: (00) 852 2356 733
Email: nbk@cih.org.hk

CIH – Careers
Tel: 024 7685 1788
Email: careers@cih.org

CIH – Distance Learning Centre
Tel: 024 7685 1789
Fax: 024 7669 4209
Email: dlc@cih.org

CIH – Education
Tel: 024 7685 1776
Fax: 024 7646 4928
Email: education@cih.org

CIH – Training England
Tel: 024 7685 1772
Fax: 024 7642 1973
Email: training.conference@cih.org

Chartered Institute of Public Finance
and Accountancy
3 Robert Street
London WC2N 6RL

Tel: 020 7543 5600
Fax: 020 7543 5700
Email: first.lastname@cipfa.org.uk
Web: www.cipfa.org.uk/

Child Poverty Action Group
94 White Lion Street
London N1 9PF
Tel: 020 7837 7979
Fax: 020 7837 6414
Email: staff@cpag.demon.co.uk
Web: www.cpag.org.uk/

Commission for Racial Equality
Elliot House
10–12 Allington Street
London SW1E 5EH
Tel: 020 7828 7022
Fax: 020 7630 7605
Email: info@cre.gov.uk
Web: www.cre.gov.uk/

Communities Scotland
91 Haymarket Terrace
Edinburgh EH12 5HE
Tel: 0131 313 0044
Fax: 0131 313 2680
Web: www.communitiesscotland.gov.uk

Crisis
1st Floor
Warwick House
25–27 Buckingham Palace Road
London SW1W OPP
Tel: 08700 113335
Email: firstname.lastname@crisis. org.uk
Web: www.crisis.org.uk

Department for Social Development
for Northern Ireland
Churchill House
Victoria Square
Belfast BT1 4SD
Tel: 028 9056 9100
Web: www.dsdni.gov.uk

Empty Homes Agency
195–197 Victoria Street
London SW1E 5NE
Tel: 020 7828 6288
Fax: 020 7828 7006
Email: info@emptyhomes.com
Web: www.emptyhomes.com

Equal Opportunities Commission
Arndale House
Arndale Centre
Manchester M4 3EQ
Tel: 0845 601 5901
Fax: 0161 838 8312
Email: info@eoc.org.uk
Web: www.eoc.org.uk/

Federation of Black Housing
Organisations
2nd Floor
1 King Edwards Road
London E9 7SF
Tel: 020 8533 7053
Fax: 020 8985 9166
Email: fbho@teleregion.co.uk

The Foyer Federation
Second Floor
Humatt House
146–148 Clerkenwell Road
London EC1R 5DG
Tel: 020 7833 8616
Fax: 020 7833 8717
Email: federation@foyer.net
Web: www.foyer.net

Help the Aged
207–221 Pentonville Road
London N1 9UZ
Tel: 020 7278 1114
Fax: 020 7278 1116
Email: info@helptheaged.org.uk
Web: www.helptheaged.org.uk/

Homeless International
Queens House

16 Queens Road
Coventry CV1 3DF
Tel: 024 7663 2802
Fax: 024 7663 2911
Email: info@homeless-international. org
Web: www.homeless-international.org/

Homeless Link
Alliance House
12 Caxton Street
London SW1H 0QS
Tel: 020 7799 2404
Fax: 020 7976 7248
Email: hn@homelesslink.org.uk
Web: www.homelesslink.org.co.uk

HOMES (Housing Organisations
Mobility and Exchange Services)
242 Vauxhall Bridge Road
London SW1V 1AU
Tel: 020 7963 0200
Fax: 020 7963 0249
Email: customer.services@homes.org.uk
Web: www.homes.org.uk/

HouseMark Online Services Ltd
Unit 8 Mercia Business Village
Torwood Close
Westwood Business Park
Coventry CV4 8HX
Tel: 024 7646 0500
Fax: 024 7646 0093
Email: info@housemark.co.uk
Web: www.housemark.co.uk

Housing Corporation (England)
Corporate Services
Maple House
149 Tottenham Court Road
London W1T 7BN
Tel: 020 7393 2000
Fax: 020 7393 2111
Email:
enquiries@housingcorp.gsx.gov.uk
Web: www.housingcorp.gov.uk/

Housing Law Practitioners
Association
120 Wilton Road
London SW1V 1JZ
Tel: 020 7233 8322
Fax: 020 7233 7779
Email: profbriefings@msn.com
Web: www.profbriefings.co.uk/assoc/
hlpa.htm

Independent Housing Ombudsman Ltd
Norman House
105–109 Strand
London WC2R 0AA
Tel: 020 7836 3630
Fax: 020 7836 3900
Email: ombudsman@ihos.org.uk
Web: www.ihos.org.uk/

Institute of Maintenance and Building
Management
Keets House
30 East Street
Farnham
Surrey GU9 7SW
Tel: 01252 710994
Fax: 01252 737741
Email: imbm@btconnect.com
Web: www.imbm.org.uk/

Institute of Residential Property
Management
178 Battersea Park Road
London SW11 4ND
Tel: 020 7622 5092
Fax: 020 7498 6153
Email: info@irpm.org.uk
Web: www.irpm.org.uk

Joseph Rowntree Foundation
The Homestead
40 Water End
York YO30 6WP
Tel: 01904 629241
Fax: 01904 620072

Email: info@jrf.org.uk
Web: www.jrf.org.uk/

Learning and Skills Council HQ
101 Lockhurst Lane
Foleshill
Coventry CV6 5SF
Tel: 0845 019 4170
Web: www.lsc.gov.uk

Leasehold Advisory Service
70–74 City Road
London EC1Y 2BJ
Tel: 020 7490 9580
Fax: 020 7253 2043
Email: info@lease-advice.org
Web: www.lease-advice.org.uk

Local Government Association
Local Government House
Smith Square
London SW1P 3HZ
Tel: 020 7664 3000
Fax: 020 7664 3030
Email: info@lga.gov.uk
Web: www.lga.gov.uk/

London Housing Unit
Association of London Government
59 and a half Southwark Street
London SE1 0AL
Tel: 020 7934 9811
Email: info-lhu@alg.gov.uk
Web: www.lhu.org.uk/

London Voluntary Service Council
356 Holloway Road
London N7 6PA
Tel: 020 7700 8107
Fax: 020 7700 8108
Minicom: 020 7700 8163
Information service and library tel:
020 7700 8104
Email: lvsc@lvsc.org.uk
Web: www.lvsc.org.uk

Mencap
123 Golden Lane
London EC1Y 0RT
Tel: 020 7454 0454
Fax: 020 7696 5540
Email: information@mencap.org.uk
Web: www.mencap.org.uk

Mencap Cymru
31 Lambourne Crescent
Cardiff Business Park
Llanishen
Cardiff CF14 5GF
Tel: 029 2074 7588
Fax: 029 2074 7550
Email: information.wales@mencap.
org.uk

Mencap in Northern Ireland
Segal House
4 Annadale Avenue
Belfast BT7 3JH
Tel: 028 9069 1351
Fax: 028 9064 0121
Email: mencapni@mencap.org.uk

Mind
15–19 Broadway
London E15 4BQ
Tel: 020 8519 2122
Fax: 020 8522 1725
Email: contact@mind.org.uk
Web: www.mind.org.uk

NACRO – National Association for
the Care and Resettlement of
Offenders
169 Clapham Road
London SW9 0PU
Tel: 020 7582 6500
Fax: 020 7735 4666
Email: firstname.lastname@nacro.org.uk
Web: www.nacro.org.uk/

National Assembly for Wales
Housing
Cathays Park
Cardiff CF10 3NQ
Tel: 029 2082 5111
Fax: 029 2092 5136
Web: www.wales.gov.uk

National Association of Citizens
Advice Bureaux
115/123 Pentonville Road
London N1 9LZ
Tel: 020 7833 2181
Fax: 020 7833 4371
Email: firstname.lastname@nacab.org.uk
Web: www.nacab.org.uk/

National Council for Voluntary
Organisations (NCVO)
Regent's Wharf
8 All Saints Street
London N1 9RL
Tel: 020 7713 6161
Fax: 020 7713 6300
Minicom: 0800 018 8111
Helpdesk: 0800 279 8798
Email: ncvo@ncvo-vol.org.uk
Web: www.ncvo-vol.org.uk

National Housing Federation
175 Gray's Inn Road
London WC1X 8UP
Tel: 020 7278 6571
Fax: 020 7833 8323
Email: info@housing.org.uk
Web: www.housing.org.uk/

National Wardens Association
Katepwa House
Ashfield Park Avenue
Ross-on-Wye
Herefordshire HR9 5AX
Tel: 01989 566699
Fax: 01989 567676
Email: nwa@assocmanagement.co.uk

Northern Ireland Federation of
Housing Associations
38 Hill Street
Belfast BT1 2LB
Tel: 028 9023 0446
Fax: 028 9023 8057
Email: info@nifha.org
Web: www.nifha.org/

Northern Ireland Housing Executive
The Housing Centre
2 Adelaide Street
Belfast BT2 8PB
Tel: 028 9024 0588
Fax: 028 9031 8008
Email: info@nihe.gov.uk
Web: www.nihe.gov.uk/

Northern Ireland Office
Block B, Castle Buildings
Belfast BT4 3SG
Tel: 028 9052 0700
Fax: 028 9052 8195
Email: press.nio@nics.gov.uk
Web: www.nio.gov.uk/

Northern Ireland Tenants Action
Project (NITAP)
PO Box 131
Ballymena BT43 6BD
Tel: 028 2564 5676
Fax: 028 2564 9729
Email: info@nitap.org
Web: www.nitap.org

Office of the Deputy Prime Minister
Eland House
Bressenden Place
London SW1E 5DU
Tel: 020 7944 4400
Email: subject@odpm.gsi.gov.uk
Web: www.odpm.gov.uk

PATH National (Positive Action for
Training in Housing)
Whittington House
764–768 Holloway Road
London N19 3JG
Tel: 020 7281 8001
Email: name@pathuk.co.uk

People for Action
3rd Floor
Queensway House
57 Livery Street
Birmingham B3 1HA
Tel: 0121 233 9003
Fax: 0121 233 9330
Email: info@pfanet.org.uk
Web: www.peopleforaction.org.uk

Property Housing and Facilities
Management Skills
Room 80
Ruskin Chambers
191 Corporation Street
Birmingham B4 6RP
Tel: 0870 241 6353
Fax: 0121 200 2889
Email: info@housingpotential.com

Property Managers Association
Scotland Ltd
2 Blythswood Square
Glasgow G2 4AD
Tel: 0141 248 4672
Fax: 0141 221 9270
Email: Jamie.millar@morisonbishop.
co.uk

Qualifications and Curriculum
Authority
83 Piccadilly
London W1J 8QA
Tel: 020 7509 5555
Fax: 020 7509 6944
Web: www.qca.org.uk/

The Rent Service
Headquarters and Policy
1st Floor
Clifton House
87–113 Euston Road
London NW1 2RA
Tel: 020 7554 2450
Web: www.therentservice.gov.uk

Royal Institution of Chartered
Surveyors (RICS)
12 Great George Street
Parliament Square
London SW1P 3AD
Tel: 020 7222 7000
Fax: 020 7222 9430
Email: info@rics.org.uk
Web: www.rics.org

Royal National Institute for the Blind
(RNIB)
105 Judd Street
London WC1H 9NE
Tel: 020 7388 1266
Fax: 020 7388 2034
Email: name@rnib.org.uk
Web: www.rnib.org.uk

RNIB Cymru
Trident Court
East Moors Road
Cardiff CF24 5TD
Tel: 029 2045 0440
Fax: 029 2044 9550

RNIB Scotland
Dunedin House
25 Ravelston Terrace
Edinburgh EH4 3TP
Tel: 0131 311 8500
Fax: 0131 311 8529

RNIB Services Northern Ireland
Unit B, 40 Linenhall Street
Belfast BT2 8BG

Tel: 028 9032 9373
Fax: 028 9043 9118

Royal National Institute for the Deaf
(RNID)
19–23 Featherstone Street
London EC1Y 8SL
Tel: 020 7296 8000
Textphone: 020 7296 8001
Fax: 020 7296 8199
Email: informationline@rnid.org.uk
Web: www.rnid.org.uk

Rural Housing Trust
8 Graphite Square
Vauxhall Walk
London SE11 5EE
Tel: 020 7793 8114
Fax: 020 7793 8148
Email: info@ruralhousing.org.uk
Web: www.ruralhousing.org.uk

Scope
6 Market Road
London N7 9PW
Tel: 020 7619 7100
Email: name@scope.org.uk
Web: www.scope.org.uk

Scottish Council for Single Homeless
5th Floor
Wellgate House
200 Cowgate
Edinburgh EH1 1NQ
Tel: 0131 226 4382
Fax: 0131 225 4382
Email: enquiries@scsh.demon.co.uk
Web: www.scsh.co.uk/

Scottish Federation of Housing
Associations
38 York Place
Edinburgh EH1 3HU
Tel: 0131 556 5777
Fax: 0131 557 6028

Email: sfha@sfha.co.uk
Web: www.sfha.co.uk/

Scottish Qualifications Authority
Hanover House
24 Douglas Street
Glasgow G2 7NQ
Tel: 0141 242 2214
Fax: 0141 242 2244
Email: helpdesk@sqa.org.uk
Web: www.sqa.org.uk/

Sense
11–13 Clifton Terrace
Finsbury Park
London N4 3SR
Tel: 020 7272 7774
Fax: 020 7272 6012
Minicom: 020 7272 9648
Email: enquiries@sense.org.uk
Web: www.sense.org.uk

Sense Cymru
5 Raleigh Walk
Brigantine Place
Atlantic Wharf
Cardiff CF10 4LN
Tel: 029 2045 7641
Fax: 029 2049 9644
Minicom: 029 2046 4125

Sense Northern Ireland
Sense Family Centre
The Manor House
51 Mallusk Road
Mallusk
County Antrim BT36 4RU
Tel: 028 9083 3430
Fax: 028 9084 4232
Minicom: 028 9083 3430

Sense Scotland
5th Floor
45 Finnieston Street
Glasgow G3 8JU

Tel: 0141 564 2444
Fax: 0141 564 2443
Minicom: 0141 564 2442
Email: info@sensescotland.org.uk
Web: www.sensescotland.org.uk

Shelter
88 Old Street
London EC1V 9HU
Tel: 020 7505 4699
Email: info@shelter.org.uk
Web: www.shelter.org.uk/

Shelter (Cymru)
25 Walter Road
Swansea
West Glamorgan SA1 5NN
Tel: 01792 469400
Fax: 01792 460050
Web: www.sheltercymru.org.uk/

Shelter (Scotland)
4th Floor
Scotiabank House
6 South Charlotte Street
Edinburgh EH2 4AW
Tel: 0131 473 7170
Fax: 0131 473 7199
Email: shelterscot@shelter.org.uk
Web: www.shelterscotland.org.uk/

Small Landlords' Association
Tel: 020 7828 2445

Tenant Participation Advisory Service
(TPAS) (England)
Brunswick House
Broad Street
Salford M6 5BZ
Tel: 0161 745 7903
Fax: 0161 745 9259
Email: info@tpas.org.uk
Web: www.tpas.org.uk/

TPAS (Cymru)
Second Floor
Transport House
1 Cathedral Road
Cardiff CF11 9SD
Tel: 029 2023 7303
Fax: 029 2034 5597
Email: enquiries@tpascymru.org.uk
Web: www.tpascymru.org.uk/

TPAS (Scotland)
74/78 Saltermarket
Glasgow G1 5LD
Tel: 0141 552 3633
Fax: 0141 552 0073

UNISON
1 Mabledon Place
London WC1H 9AJ
Tel: 020 7388 2366
Fax: 020 7387 6692
Email: initial.surname@unison.org.uk
Web: www.unison.org.uk/

Welsh Federation of Housing
Associations
Norbury House
Norbury Road
Fairwater
Cardiff CF5 3AS
Tel: 029 2030 3150
Fax: 029 2056 0668
Email: wfha@welshhousing.org.uk
Web: www.welshhousing.org.uk/

Welsh Local Government Association
Local Government House
Drake Walk
Cardiff CF10 4LG
Tel: 029 2046 8600
Fax: 029 2046 8601
Email: info@wlga.gov.uk
Web: www.wlga.gov.uk/

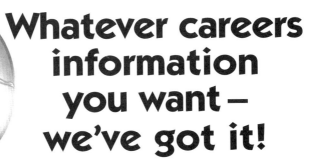

NOTES